COMMUNIST CONTINUITY AND THE FIGHT FOR WOMEN'S LIBERATION

Part 2

Women, Leadership, and the Proletarian Norms of the Communist Movement

PATHFINDER
New York   London   Montreal   Sydney

Contents

Introduction	4
by Mary-Alice Waters, July 26, 1992	
1. Confronting the leadership pressures on women during a retreat of the labor movement	9
Report on 'Preparing the election of the National Committee,' adopted by SWP National Committee, May 1985	
by Mary-Alice Waters	
Reprinted from Information Bulletin *no. 2 in 1985, June 1985*	
2. Forging the leadership of a proletarian party	34
Excerpt from report adopted by SWP National Committee, May 1979	
by Mary-Alice Waters	
Reprinted from SWP Discussion Bulletin, *vol. 36, no. 13, July 1979*	
3. Leading the party into industry	50
Excerpt from report adopted by SWP National Committee, February 1978	
by Jack Barnes	
Reprinted from Party Organizer, *vol. 2, no. 2, April 1978*	
4. Violence against women is incompatible with party membership	60
Excerpt from 'Political Committee report on Control Commission recommendations,' report adopted by SWP National Convention, August 13, 1977	
by Linda Jenness	
Reprinted from Internal Information Bulletin *no. 7 in 1977, September 1977*	
5. Communist norms and nonexclusive social affairs	63
Report adopted by SWP National Convention, August 13, 1977	
by Catarino Garza	
Reprinted from Internal Information Bulletin *no. 7 in 1977, September 1977*	
6. Race-baiting and communist leadership	68
Report adopted by SWP National Committee, February 1986	
by Mac Warren	
Reprinted from Information Bulletin *no. 1 in 1986, April 1986*	
7. Children, child care, and membership norms of a proletarian party	76
Report adopted by SWP Political Committee, June 18, 1986	
by Jack Barnes	
Reprinted from Information Bulletin *no. 2 in 1986, August 1986*	

Appendix 1
Letter to Political Committee from James, June 12, 1986   **88**
Letter to Political Committee from Vivian, June 6, 1986   **91**
   Reprinted from Information Bulletin *no. 2 in 1986, August 1986*

Appendix 2
Excerpt from report on women's liberation movement   **94**
From report adopted by SWP National Committee, March 14, 1971
by Betsey Stone
   Reprinted from Internal Information Bulletin *no. 2 in 1971, April 1971*

Introduction

by Mary-Alice Waters

From Wichita to Buffalo, from Boston to Milwaukee, from New Orleans to New York, a new generation of women is taking to the streets to defend women's rights. A new fighting layer of the working class is learning to see the defense of these rights as inseparable from defending the democratic rights of all and the class interests of workers.

As thousands of women come to recognize the need to *act* to prevent hard-fought gains from being lost, they are rejecting the myth that the oppression of women as a sex was vanquished by the "second wave" of the feminist movement in the early 1970s. They are confronting all the fundamental questions that previous generations of women fighting for their liberation have addressed, and that the working-class vanguard must answer if it is to advance toward socialism.

Why are women oppressed? How did that oppression begin? Why are opponents of a woman's right to choose and of the Equal Rights Amendment so determined to perpetuate laws and customs that deny women an equal role in society? Who benefits? What social forces have the power to end the second-class status of women, and have common interests in the fight for women's liberation?

These three Education for Socialists bulletins—which bear the common title *Communist Continuity and the Fight for Women's Liberation: Documents of the Socialist Workers Party, 1971–86*—aim to make available raw materials that will help the generation of women and men now joining battle in defense of women's rights find the answers to these and similar questions and win them to the communist movement.

The bulletins should be read as a "work in progress." They draw together in one place some of the most important resolutions, reports, and articles that come out of the active involvement of the Socialist Workers Party and Young Socialist Alliance in the fight for women's rights since a new feminist movement arose at the end of the 1960s. A product of the deep-going economic and social changes that began with Washington's preparations for entry into World War II, the "second wave" of feminism was one of the powerful components of the radicalization of the 1960s and 1970s that profoundly affected the working class and changed political consciousness on an even broader scale.

Part I of the series, *Women's Liberation and the Line of March of the Working Class*, contains the main programmatic documents, or articles and reports based on them, that have been adopted by the Socialist Workers Party since 1979. Central to this bulletin is the resolution "Socialist Revolution and the Struggle for Women's Liberation," adopted by the SWP convention in August 1979. The resolution in its final form was the product of collective discussion and debate in the international movement the SWP was part of at that time, the Fourth International, and is enriched by the varied experiences in many countries it incorporates. The initial drafting of the resolution, however, as well as the final editing, was done by the leadership of the SWP. While one or two points would be developed differently if written today, and others added, the resolution remains the best guide we have on the central place and weight of the fight for women's liberation in the strategic line of march of the working class toward socialism.

Other materials in Part I develop specific points that are incorporated in the international resolution. The excerpts from other reports often explain at greater length or more clearly how we arrived at some of the conclusions that are codified in the resolution.

"The Capitalist Ideological Offensive against Women Today" builds on the international resolution to take up a number of important questions that came to the fore in the early 1980s. It is excerpted from the introduction to the book *Cosmetics, Fashions, and the Exploitation of Women;* that introduction was based on a report adopted by the SWP National Committee entitled "Confronting the Leadership Pressures on Women during a Retreat of the Labor Movement," which is contained in Part II of this series.

All of the material in Part I registers the political conquests of the SWP since the late 1970s, as the party cadres deepened their orientation toward the industrial working class and unions, building a party that is proletarian not only in its program and perspectives but overwhelmingly in its composition, political milieu, and rhythms of activity as well. As part of that process, deepening our understanding of the character and central importance of the fight to end women's oppression as a sex was indispensable.

Reading this material together with the SWP resolutions and reports contained in *The Changing Face of U.S. Politics: The Proletarian Party and the Trade Unions,* published by Pathfinder Press, will place it in an even broader national and international class framework. The women involved in the work documented in these bulletins were the same women who were advancing the fights in their plants and unions and in the broader working-class movement. And they were changing themselves and their party in the process.

The documents in Part II, *Women, Leadership, and Proletarian Norms of the Communist Movement,* register the party's political progress as we conquered the kinds of working-class attitudes and norms of functioning that make it possible for workers, members of oppressed nationalities, and women to develop as party leaders. The ability of the Socialist Workers Party cadres to discuss objectively and lead politically on the range of questions documented here has been unique in the communist movement. These questions include:

- the need for affirmative action within the party;
- why quotas, exclusive caucuses, and exclusionary social activities are destructive to comradely relations and leadership development in a revolutionary centralist working-class organization;
- eradicating the cancer of race-baiting;
- establishing that violence of any kind against women destroys party democracy and political equality and is incompatible with membership;
- helping members with children maximize their political activity, without pretending the party can or should take responsibility for child care.

The SWP has conquered these proletarian norms and rejected the petty-bourgeois attitudes and functioning prevalent in other organizations that pretend to speak in the interests of the working class. Had we not been able to do so, the SWP too would have been torn apart in petty factional battles and clique fights similar to those that have decimated the Communist Party, among others, in recent years.

Part III of the series is entitled *Abortion Rights, the ERA, and the Rebirth of a Feminist Movement: The Party Campaigns for Women's Rights.* It contains the resolution adopted by the SWP in 1971, the first party convention after the mass movement for women's liberation burst on the political scene; it registers the party's enthusiastic support for, and involvement in, that revolutionary development. While this might seem unremarkable today, at the time it set the SWP apart from virtually all other working-class organizations.

Part III also contains "Feminism and the Marxist Movement," which took up and answered the challenge of the "socialist-feminist" currents that emerged as part of the new radicalization. These currents decried the supposed theoretical inadequacies of Marxism and argued the need for a new theoretical framework to chart a course toward women's liberation.

The core of Part III, however, documents the work of the Socialist Workers Party and Young Socialist Alliance to build the abortion rights movement in the early 1970s and, a few years later, to mobilize the kind of movement that would have been necessary to win the Equal Rights Amendment to the U.S. Constitution. These reports and articles draw together the work we were part of and capture the campaigning, interventionist spirit of the party and youth; they provide the best guide for today, as we respond to the new struggles that are unfolding.

As we collectively read, study, discuss, and use this material, we will gain a better appreciation of what is most valuable in preparing us to participate in today's struggles. We will also better understand the accomplishments and conquests of the battles that have brought us this far.

In bringing these documents together, no attempt has been made to edit them in light of later experience or to change formulations or points in early documents that are clarified and explained more accurately in later materials. Readers will be able to see for themselves the evolution of the party's collective thinking and growing political comprehension of a range of questions.

JULY 26, 1992

Contents of Part I

Part I—Women's liberation and the line of march of the working class

Introduction
by Mary-Alice Waters, July 26, 1992

1. **The capitalist ideological offensive against women today**
   Excerpt from introduction to Cosmetics, Fashions, and the Exploitation of Women
   by Mary-Alice Waters, November 1985

2. **The struggle by women against their oppression as a sex is a form of the class struggle**
   Report adopted by the National Convention of the Socialist Workers Party, August 7, 1979
   by Mary-Alice Waters
   Reprinted from International Internal Discussion Bulletin, *vol. XVI, no. 6, October 1979*

3. **Socialist revolution and the struggle for women's liberation**
   Resolution adopted by the National Convention of the Socialist Workers Party, August 7, 1979
   Reprinted from 1979 World Congress of the Fourth International: Major resolutions and reports, *special supplement to* Intercontinental Press

4. **Social weight and revolutionary strategy for the transformation of the labor movement**
   Excerpt from report adopted by SWP National Committee, April 29, 1979
   by Jack Barnes
   From 'A new stage of revolutionary working-class politics,' from Part II: 'The roots of revolutionary strategy.' Reprinted from The Changing Face of U.S. Politics: The Proletarian Party and the Trade Unions

5. **Affirmative action gains for women in industry and the way forward for the women's movement**
   Excerpt from report adopted by SWP National Committee, April 29, 1979
   by Jack Barnes
   From 'A new stage of revolutionary working-class politics,' from Part III: 'Resolving the crisis of proletarian leadership.' Reprinted from The Changing Face of U.S. Politics: The Proletarian Party and the Trade Unions

Contents of Part III

Part III—Abortion rights, the ERA, and the rebirth of a feminist movement: The party campaigns for women's rights

1. **The abortion struggle: What have we accomplished; where should we go from here?**
   by Betsey Stone and Mary-Alice Waters
   Reprinted from SWP Discussion Bulletin, *vol. 31, no. 19, July 1973*

2. **Feminism and the Marxist movement**
   by Mary-Alice Waters
   Reprinted from Pathfinder pamphlet; originally published in October 1972 International Socialist Review

3. **Toward a mass feminist movement**
   Resolution adopted by SWP National Convention, August 1971
   Reprinted from SWP Discussion Bulletin, *vol. 29, no. 4, April 1971*

4. **Emergence of a new feminist movement**
   Excerpt from 'Perspectives and Lessons of the New Radicalization,' political resolution adopted by the SWP National Convention, August 1971
   Reprinted from A Revolutionary Strategy for the 70s: Documents of the Socialist Workers Party

5. **Struggles by women reflect the depth of the social crisis and radicalization**
   Excerpts from 'Prospects for Socialism in America,' political resolution adopted by SWP National Convention, August 1975
   Reprinted from The Changing Face of U.S. Politics: The Proletarian Party and the Trade Unions
   From Part IV: 'Changing Character and Composition of the Working Class'
   From Part V: 'Radicalization and Mobilization of the Allies of the Proletariat'

6. **The fight for an independent women's movement**
   Report adopted by SWP National Committee, February 25, 1978, by Willie Mae Reid
   Reprinted from Party Organizer, vol. 2, no. 3, May 1978

   ### Appendix: April 1977 National NOW Conference
   2,000 feminists debate strategy for movement, by Nancy Cole
   Reprinted from the Militant, *May 6, 1977*
   SWP answers red-baiting, by Mary-Alice Waters
   Reprinted from the Militant, *May 6, 1977*

7. **Campaigning for the ERA**

   (a) **Impact of July 9, 1978, 100,000-strong march on Washington for the ERA and the perspectives for NOW**
   Report adopted by SWP Political Bureau, November 3, 1978, by Wendy Lyons
   Reprinted from Party Organizer, vol. 2, no. 8, November 1978

   (b) **Labor for Equal Rights Now (LERN) and the Illinois ERA campaign**
   Report adopted by SWP national steelworkers fraction, February 24, 1980, by Pat Grogan
   Reprinted from Party Organizer, vol. 4, no. 1, April 1980

   (c) **Mortal blow to the ERA: NOW leadership capitulates to Washington's third militarization drive**
   Excerpt from report on 'Imperialist Militarization and the Draft,' adopted by SWP National Committee, May 25, 1980, by Andrea Morell
   Reprinted from Party Organizer, vol. 5, no. 2, April 1981

CONFRONTING THE LEADERSHIP PRESSURES ON WOMEN DURING A RETREAT OF THE LABOR MOVEMENT
Report on 'Preparing the election of the National Committee'
Adopted by SWP National Committee, May 1985

by Mary-Alice Waters

One of the responsibilities of the convention of the Socialist Workers Party to be held in August is the election of a new National Committee.

The Political Committee proposes that this National Committee meeting adopt a number of proposals to guide the delegates who will be discussing nominations in branch delegation meetings prior to the convention, serving on the Nominations Commission, and electing the new NC at the final session of the convention. These guidelines should be presented to the delegates at the opening session of the convention and discussed prior to the election of the Nominations Commission. The proposals adopted by the convention will guide the work of the commission.

We propose:

1) That there be no change in the size of the National Committee at this convention.

2) That the convention use alternate membership on the National Committee, especially the bottom two-thirds of the list, to bring onto the NC a substantial number of comrades who are not currently members. This should include both younger party members who have demonstrated their potential to develop as future party leaders, and comrades who, regardless of age, are currently playing a leadership role in branches and fractions across the country. The purpose is to give such comrades, irrespective of previous membership on the committee, the opportunity to go through a year or two's experience as NC members, allowing the party to further test them as well as benefit from their experience.

3) That we reaffirm and apply our general leadership criteria in the election of the National Committee. By this we mean that the party neither has quotas on the NC for comrades who are oppressed under capitalism for reasons of class, race, or sex; nor do we turn a blind-eye to the reality of this oppression or ignore our responsibility to take special measures to encourage such comrades to realize their full leadership potential.

The process of leadership development takes place daily in the branches, fractions, and in the mass movement. We lead the party by helping *every* comrade carry out varied assignments and learn from her or his experiences. In this framework, we consciously act in such a way as to give special encouragement to working class comrades. This fundamental long-term class goal guides us to pay particular attention to helping comrades of the oppressed nationalities and women comrades to overcome the greater obstacles they must surmount to become confident, rounded, political leaders of a multinational proletarian party. The success of this affirmative action is registered in the election of the National Committee.

These proposals build on, and if implemented will enable us to move forward from, the substantial accomplishment made by our last constitutional convention in August 1984. The delegates to that convention reduced the size of the National Committee by roughly 40 percent. This both (1) brought it into harmony with the current size of the party, and (2) established a committee of a workable size.

That step was a real test of the objectivity and political consciousness of the entire party. The proposal was discussed at two NC meetings, and then adopted by the NC. It was discussed by each branch delegation when it met to consider nominations for the NC to be made to the convention.

Despite the nomination of many more than 50 capable comrades, not one single delegate either in the Nominations Commission or on the convention floor proposed that the committee should be larger than the 50 members recommended by the outgoing National Committee. That single fact clearly indicates how well the party understood and agreed with the need to make the change in the size of the National Committee.

We should note another fact, as well. The National Committee led the party in making this change. We tend to take this for granted, but we shouldn't. Subjectivity, not objectivity, often comes to the fore when questions of leadership "posts" and "recognition" are under discussion. I have seen similar proposals evoke very heated divisions in the leadership of other sections of the Fourth International. The starting point is not always an objective assessment of the needs of the organization, but often a narrow and subjective response focused on what such a proposal means for me, for my tendency, my faction, my clique.

That was not what happened in our National Committee. The NC responded objectively, thinking of the party's needs, not "me," "my role," or "our committee." The NC said to the party, we will have a better committee and a better leadership structure as a whole, one that better suits the needs of the party, if 50 percent of us, more or less, are not elected to the incoming National Committee. Not because 50 percent of us are no longer qualified to be on a National Committee, but because the size of the committee is no longer in line with the party's needs. In doing this the National Committee members demonstrated one of the most important qualities of leadership—the capacity to see themselves in relation to the party, rather than looking at the party in relation to themselves.

Being elected to the National Committee doesn't make anyone a leader, any more than not being elected to the NC means someone isn't a leader. It's an additional responsibility for those elected. But leadership isn't defined by membership on any committee, or any post. It is how you carry out your assignment whatever it may be, how you organize others to work together, how you help others to become leaders.

Emphasizing that membership on any particular body is not what defines leadership, of course, does not mean that the leadership committees are unimportant or that membership on them is irrelevant. To the contrary, revolutionary centralism assumes a structured, disciplined leadership to politically organize the party. These democratically elected leadership committees have enormous weight, and their functioning is decisive in a Marxist party.

The lead taken by the National Committee to reduce the size of the NC facilitated similar adjustments on other leadership bodies, including branch, local, district, and state executive committees. The decision made by the National Committee last December that we didn't need to continue having several elected chairpersons of the party provided yet another small example of how we approach questions of leadership. [See report on "Dissolving the Office of National Chairpersons of the Socialist Workers Party," *Information Bulletin,* No. 2 in 1985.]

The end of a process, not the beginning

The accomplishment registered in the election of the NC at the 1984 convention was the end of a process, however, not the beginning. It was a turning point, a kind of watershed. The adjustment we made created the preconditions to move forward. We were dropping the curtain on a whole previous period. We had to bring the size of the National Committee into harmony with the size of the party before we could have an accurate picture of ourselves, before we could see where we really were in the development of the party leadership. We had to take that step before we could once again review, and once again concentrate on implementing, the criteria that guide us in electing a National Committee.

We are not saying that the leadership committees elected at the last few conventions were inadequate. To the contrary, they were the correct leadership committees for the party at that time. The report adopted by the opening session of the convention last year reviews this evolution of the NC in relationship to the party from a different angle than we will be discussing at this meeting, and comrades will find it useful to consider the two reports together.

The last convention was, roughly speaking, the culmination of a substantial period of adjustment and change that began with the turn, some seven years ago. Between 1978 and 1984 we succeeded in leading the overwhelming majority of the party into industry and into the industrial unions, changing the axis and milieu of the party and establishing a new and stable framework for building the multinational revolutionary cadre of a proletarian party.

We accomplished this during a period in which the party was slowly declining in membership under the pressures of a strong and concerted ruling-class offensive against the working class on all fronts. There is now evidence that the departures have slowed down, and that recruitment has begun to accelerate, so that over the last year the two processes have more or less offset each other. That is certainly a welcome development. Before the last convention, however, our leadership structures were too large for a party in the range of 800 to 1,200 members. They were still those of a party in the range of 1,500 to 2,000.

When the leadership structure is out of balance with the size of the party, that inevitably affects our political functioning. Moreover, all kinds of broad leadership questions are simply sloughed over because they are not clearly posed. We were like a person wearing a pair of pants that is three sizes too large. Since the pants are too big anyway, you can put on a few pounds, lose a few pounds, and never have to face up to the facts. When there is a lot of slack, you can avoid taking a hard look at what is happening in the leadership, especially on questions such as what progress is being made in the development of leaders who are Black, who are women, who are newly recruited workers (or farmers), who are young.

Just prior to the last convention we made some real mistakes in a number of branches on leadership questions. We started to abdicate responsibility for *leading* on these matters. We discussed this at the opening session of the convention in August 1984, and began correcting ourselves, as comrades can see from the report printed in this bulletin. A good many branch delegations had simply sidestepped the responsibility of seriously talking out and deciding on nominations for the National Committee.

The National Committee as a whole had not done its job either. NC members in a number of branches had not participated in the delegation meetings, sometimes arguing mistakenly that it would be more "democratic" if they stood aside and let other delegates lead on this particular question.

The result in at least one branch was a decision to not even discuss the merits of various nominations for the NC, nor to rank them, but simply to renominate everyone on the outgoing committee, plus whomever else the delegates thought deserved consideration. The National Committee was thus unwittingly elevated into a "House of Lords," whose members deserved nomination simply because they had previously been elected to the NC. Their performance relative to other nominees was not subject to evaluation by the comrades with whom they were working most closely. This, of course, was not the intent, but it was one result of our getting sloppy, and lazy, on leadership questions. It was one more indication of the pressing need to make the adjustment we did in the size and functioning of the NC.

Two challenges
The leadership questions discussed and the decisions we made at the last convention laid the foundations for taking up the tasks that are before us now. The delegates to the 1985 convention will have to address different questions.

The challenge is not to redress a weakness that has already emerged. That has been the case at some previous conventions, but this year we see no big problems that need corrective action by the delegates. It is more a case of looking ahead to avoid sliding into potential mistakes that would be easy to make, given the pressures of the political conditions in which we are building the party today.

There are two such potential problems that we need to talk out in preparation for the convention.

The first challenge is to avoid drifting toward a frozen National Committee. It would be a mistake, and a real weakness, if we went through several conventions that resulted in little change, little renewal, in the National Committee. This would be a weakening of our continuity.

The second challenge is to avoid drifting toward de facto quotas on the National Committee for comrades who are women and for comrades of the oppressed nationalities. We need instead to continue to implement our general approach to leadership development, including our affirmative action norms. The degree of our success in this leadership development will be registered in the election of the NC.

Both of these potential problems are inherent in the kind of political period we are living through, but this doesn't mean that they are unavoidable. They are fostered by the slow pace of recruitment that we have experienced for a number of years, and by an interrelated factor: we are not living through and participating in the kinds of class battles that accelerate the pace of leadership testing and development.

If you look at the statistics on the ages and dates of recruitment for the National Committee members elected at the 1984 convention, and compare them with a similar breakdown of the NC elected in 1979, you can see some of the relevant changes wrought by the objective conditions we have faced in the last period.

There has been a reduction at both ends of the age spectrum, and both register a weakness for the party to be aware of. For instance we would be stronger if we had more Pearl Chertovs and Tom Leonards.

On the other end of the age spread, you will notice that today there is not a single regular member of the National Committee who is under 30 years old, and there are only two alternates under 30. This is quite a change for us. Even in the 1960s, for example, when an extremely high percentage of the NC was composed of comrades with decades of experience, plus another layer in their 40s and 50s, we always had a component of comrades under 30 on the National Committee.

The statistics also show the major clumps of comrades who joined under the impetus of different upsurges of class struggle and began to accumulate leadership experience in those battles.

There is a layer of comrades on the National Committee who were won to the party in the late 1950s and early 1960s—the generation of the Cuban revolution, the civil rights movement, and Malcolm X.

There is another big layer who joined toward the end of the 1960s and early 1970s. That was the period when the Vietnam antiwar movement was at its height, the Chicano movement and feminist movement were exploding, and a number of local battles over desegregation, busing, and police brutality were on the rise.

There was an upturn of recruitment among Puerto Rican, Mexicano, Chicano, and other comrades of Latin American origin in the 1976–77 period, as the bosses intensified their drive to terrorize undocumented workers and to make non-anglo workers in general more vulnerable to superexploitation. The efforts to organize resistance to these attacks brought a layer of comrades into the party and gave them broader leadership experience. This is reflected in our current National Committee.

After that, from the late 1970s on, there are no big clumps. Even the two National Committee members who have joined since 1980 are not exactly youth. We recruited Mel Mason and Joe Swanson, not their kids. Not yet, anyway. So they, too, are part of the generation whose leadership experience in the mass movement goes back through the 1970s and 1960s, even though they didn't join the party before the 1980s.

The profile of the YSA today adds another graphic component. The YSA is a youth organization in program and perspective, and in its capacity to intervene and recruit and grow. But in terms of age composition, the YSA is not predominantly a youth organization today. At the beginning of 1985, more than 50 percent of the YSA membership was 27 years of age or older, and almost 50 percent had been in the YSA four years or longer. That's a youth organization in perspective and orientation, but not in composition.

This is not because the party and YSA have been doing something wrong, however. It is not because some other political current is getting a new generation of youth while we are missing out. No, that test is coming. The current age composition of the YSA is simply another concrete indication of the kind of period we've been living through. One way we will know when the class struggle is beginning to heat up will be its reflection in stepped-up recruitment of young people to the YSA.

That's why the openings that do exist—like those around April 20, the farm protests, the South Africa demonstrations on campus and off, and the attitudes of young workers toward such actions—are so important to us. Our ability to respond to these developments and begin recruiting out of them—as reports indicated we are doing—is crucial to the health and future of the YSA and party.

On the leadership level of the party, however, which is what we are focusing on here, the statistics indicate that there is not today a burgeoning generation of newly recruited potential party leaders that, by their very numbers and level of activity, is pressuring the party to make room on the National Committee for new blood. Since there is less pressure from this direction than at some other times in the past, we need to be more conscious over the next few years about bringing onto the committee as alternate members a number of younger comrades who have proven their leadership potential.

No one should be elected to the National Committee simply because they are young. We don't have to go out and hunt for "youth" to nominate. And we have no quota we're trying to fill. If we proceed along the lines we have been discussing since our last convention, with thorough preparation by branch delegations and objective deliberations by the delegates, then whatever nominations are appropriate will come out of that process quite naturally.

What we do have to weigh carefully, however, is the choice we make when we have two nominees, for example, one of whom is 27 and the other 41. The younger comrade may be relatively less experienced and less of a leader today—not yet someone who shoulders the kind of broad leadership responsibility NC members are expected to take. But that is not the only thing to be weighed. If comrades have reason to believe that the experience of serving on the NC for a couple of years might give the younger comrade the little push necessary to advance her or him toward becoming more of a leader, then such a consideration should get some weight. That is in the best interests of the party, since, all other factors aside, the odds are that younger comrades have a few more years of activity in them than older ones. Serving on the NC is an education as well as a challenge. We have to think about the future of the party as well as the present.

Having underlined the need to be conscious about age, it is important to be explicit about another question. Otherwise the age factor will get exaggerated.

Renewal of the National Committee does not take place only through the infusion of new young leaders, and at some conventions that is not even the primary source of new blood. There is turnover among older cadres, too, among comrades who have been in the party for a good number of years, taking on varied leadership responsibilities. There is always a layer who are not on the National Committee, even though they are currently playing major leadership roles in the branches, fractions, or national apparatus.

Probably the greatest single weakness of the NC today, for example, is the degree to which it does not incorporate the real leadership of our branches. A good number of comrades who have been chosen by the executive committees of our largest branches to take on the responsibilities of a full-time organizer are not on the NC. There are other comrades with considerable leadership experience who are helping to organize national fractions, or heading up major departments of our national apparatus, and are not NC members. Of course, that is inevitable—and positive. If the leadership were not broader and larger than the National Committee, we would be in bad shape. But the party gains from assuring that a substantial proportion of comrades such as this who are leading our work today are challenged to take on even broader national responsibilities, and that we bring into our leadership deliberations this range of experience.

All of these factors should be taken into consideration in the election of the alternate members of the National Committee, especially, as outlined at the beginning of the report.

This is nothing new. It is one of the reasons our National Committee is structured as it is.

Regular membership tends to have a high degree of carry-over from one convention to the next, since it is composed in large part of the most experienced national leadership of the party. That does not mean that there are few changes in the regular members. To the contrary, there is always turnover, and at any particular convention the changes may be substantially greater than on the alternate list, reflecting real leadership evolution. But there is something different about the way we use the alternate membership.

The convention often uses the alternate list, especially after the first few rankings, to encourage and facilitate the process of incorporating new comrades into the National Committee. Thus the alternate membership always tends to change quite a bit from convention to convention. These changes do not necessarily mean that someone not reelected as an alternate is no longer functioning up to the standards of NC membership, but that the convention is acting to broaden the experience on this national leadership body among a wider layer of party leaders. Using the alternate membership in this way gives a larger cross-section of the leadership the opportunity to work as part of the National Committee and develop in that process. It also gives the party the possibility to continuously draw on and test potential leaders.

Both aspects of this are indispensable components of maintaining the continuity of the party.

This is important, because we sometimes mistakenly think of continuity as synonymous with the long-time stable leadership role of experienced cadres. But continuity is based on the stable *transmission* of accumulated knowledge and experience, and there can be no transmission without renewal and change, without the intertwining of past, present, and future. Continuity is more accurately like a rope or a chain in which new experiences and leadership cadres become intermeshed with the older, and the threads that are worn or frayed are continuously replaced.

That kind of continuity is both a precondition for a stable and authoritative leadership and vice versa. A stable and authoritative leadership is necessary to assure continuity.

Affirmative action, not quotas

The potential to drift toward a de facto quota system in the composition of the National Committee is also inherent when the pace of our recruitment is as slow as it has been. The party is proud of what we have accomplished over the last decade. We're proud of the very real advances we have made in consolidating an increasingly proletarian leadership that includes a sizeable proportion of comrades who are Black, comrades of other oppressed nationalities, and comrades who are women. This pride expresses itself in a determination not to allow the pressures and difficulties of the current period to push us back on this front.

But it's not a question of will.

If we were recruiting at a faster pace, the process of renewing the cadre that is female, Black, Chicano, Mexicano, Puerto Rican, Asian would also take place relatively normally as part of the more general development of new leadership.

But when the pace of recruitment slows down and the normal attrition of time and age take their toll, there can be a tendency toward conservatism, even unconsciously. And conservatism can inadvertently turn into fakery—into fooling ourselves. We can drift toward not renewing the committee, toward not electing new or younger comrades to the NC unless the percentages remain basically unchanged, because we don't want to start sliding back. But that turns the whole question of leadership on its head, seeing election to the NC as the means of conferring leadership status, rather than as a way that leadership development is registered.

We don't approach the election of the National Committee from the point of view of who is *not* being elected. Even less do we start with who is being taken off the outgoing committee. No one is entitled to special consideration *to stay on* the NC simply because they have been elected before; nor do comrades get special consideration *to stay on* because they are a worker, a female, or Black. If we started doing that, instead of trying to apply our leadership criteria objectively to all nominees, then we would inadvertently foster both the development of a House of Lords, and accelerate the drift toward a de facto quota system within it. Rather than electing a committee that reflects the real day-to-day leadership of the party, we would be filling slots. The end result would be a committee with diminished authority in the eyes of the party.

Leadership criteria

One of the most useful things we can do in preparing the convention is to review some of the things we've discussed and adopted in recent years concerning our leadership criteria. What is leadership in a proletarian party? Together with this report we should reprint some of the reports on this question that we've adopted in recent years, and that guide us today, so that comrades can read or reread them prior to the convention.

Here I only want to reiterate a few basic points

that are developed more thoroughly elsewhere. The 1978 report by Jack [Barnes] on "Leading the Party Into Industry," and the 1979 report that I gave on "Forging the Leadership of a Proletarian Party," are especially relevant. [See elsewhere in this bulletin.]

First, the National Committee is a *committee*. Its capacity to function as a collective political leadership is what is decisive. When the National Committee meets, do the comrades present bring into the deliberations the class-struggle experiences in which the party is involved? Is it a body that has the "capacity to lead the party in action," as Farrell Dobbs's 1971 memorandum [reprinted elsewhere in this bulletin] put it? Is it "in step with the party ranks"? Most importantly, is it a body that is capable of thinking out and making decisions on the broadest political and programmatic challenges facing the working-class vanguard?

The NC is judged by its collective ability to politically lead, not by the capacities of any individual. Whether any particular comrade should be elected to the NC at a given convention can be judged only by looking at the committee as a whole in relation to the needs of the party.

Second, the National Committee must be the real national leadership of the party. If the NC is not composed of those comrades who shoulder the broad political responsibilities of leading the party on a daily basis, then over time, it will have little authority. Nothing could destabilize the party and undermine the self-confidence of the cadres more rapidly or completely than if a gap were to develop between the real leadership and the formal leadership bodies of the party.

Another way of saying the same thing is that you don't change the leadership by electing an individual to the NC—or by not electing someone. An election per se doesn't make anyone a leader. It has nothing to do with real leadership development, except as a challenge to shoulder greater responsibility; in that sense it can nudge the process along. But election to one or another leadership committee has to be an expression of a process that has already been taking place for some time—in the branches and fractions, in the mass movement, and in the functioning of the National Committee and other leadership bodies themselves. Otherwise it's a fraud that has nothing in common with proletarian organizational norms.

Of course, no National Committee is ever perfect. There is no such thing. Each committee is the best effort at any particular convention to elect a body of a given size, composed of comrades who have shown themselves to be leaders. It is done anew each convention.

Third, the National Committee is not *the* leadership of the party. That, fortunately, is much broader than the National Committee. It is always possible to select some different individuals at any particular convention and have a good committee. Understanding this is crucial to learning to be objective about the National Committee elections, to have a sense of proportion, as Farrell used to say, about every nomination.

Fourth, while the National Committee is judged by its performance as a *committee*, by its collective functioning, the conduct of NC members as individuals inevitably becomes an element that substantially affects the authority of the committee. Respect for and a close and objective working relationship with the ranks of the party; comradely relations and loyal collaboration with other members of leadership committees to ensure that the elected leadership bodies function; the highest degree of integrity in relations with leaders and cadres of the Fourth International and its sections, as well as other revolutionary Marxist forces internationally—on all these fronts, individual National Committee members set examples of conduct that weigh heavily in the ranks of the party and international movement. They reflect on the integrity of the committee—and the party—as a whole.

That is why the party's resolution on "The Organizational Character of the Socialist Workers Party" is so explicit concerning the leadership standards that the party demands of National Committee members. Members of the National Committee have few rights, but substantial obligations and responsibilities. As the resolution states:

> To build the combat organization capable of leading the masses to power, the party must have as its general staff a corps of professional revolutionists who devote their entire life to the direction and the building of the party and its influence in the mass movement. Membership in the leading staff of the

party, the National Committee, must be made contingent on a complete subordination of the life of the candidate to the party. All members of the National Committee must be prepared to devote full-time activities to party work at the demand of the National Committee.

The party demands the greatest sacrifices of its members. Only a leadership selected from among those who demonstrate in the struggle the qualities of singleness of purpose, unconditional loyalty to the party and revolutionary firmness of character, can inspire the membership with the spirit of unswerving devotion required for victory. . . .

The membership of the party has the right to demand and expect the greatest responsibility from the leaders precisely because of the position they occupy in the movement. The selection of comrades to positions of leadership means the conferring of an extraordinary responsibility. The warrant for this position must be proved, not once, but continuously by the leadership itself. It is under obligation to set the highest example of responsibility, devotion, sacrifice and complete identification with the party itself and its daily life and action.

Fifth, the development of the party leadership demands consciousness, and, like all other aspects of political activity, it must be led. We have to work at assuring the optimum conditions for the development of the leadership necessary for the future as well as today.

A central aspect of this is an explicit norm of "affirmative action" within the party. We take special measures to support and encourage working-class comrades. We pay particular attention to helping comrades who are Black, the big majority of whom, of course, are also workers, given the class composition of the oppressed nationalities in the United States. We take similar measures in relation to comrades who are Puerto Rican and Chicano and Mexicano and Asian. We help women comrades to overcome the even greater obstacles they face in developing the confidence to be the kind of leaders required of our kind of party.

This is not a question of having different standards for young workers who join the party, Black or white, or for women. There would be nothing more demeaning or paternalistic, nothing more corrosive to the political homogeneity of the party on which the mutual confidence of comrades is founded. Moreover, there is no special road to the development of leaders who come from the ranks of the exploited classes of modern capitalist society and those specially oppressed by it.

The heart of the challenge is the deepening of our proletarian attitudes and norms aimed at encouraging *every* comrade to develop his or her potential to the fullest. No one is ever treated with ridicule or contempt, or made to feel "stupid" or uneducated, for expressing their ideas, however faltering or unsure they may initially be. That is the starting point for a communist party, a workers' party—the only kind of party in which those fighting to overcome the limitation imposed on them by capitalist oppression can develop as political leaders of a multinational proletarian party.

I always liked the way Trotsky emphasized this point in a 1937 letter he wrote to comrades here in the United States, taking up the question of proletarian versus petty-bourgeois attitudes to leadership. He noted that leadership in a revolutionary working-class party is not defined by the capacity to be glib with "general formulas and fluent pens," although that is what happens in organizations dominated by middle-class itellectuals, while workers rich in life experience and class-struggle savvy are pushed aside. The first qualification of a leader in a proletarian party, Trotsky insisted, is the capacity to listen, to hear what comrades are saying. "In the first place a good ear, and only in the second place a good tongue," was the way he put it. [See *Background to "The Struggle for a Proletarian Party,"* an Education For Socialists publication, p. 14.]

Proletarian attitudes and norms of relations within the party are the beginning of the question— and at least 90 percent of the solution—when it comes to creating the conditions in which young working-class comrades, including those of oppressed nationalities, and women can advance as self-confident leaders of our class. That is not the end of the question, however.

There is a special challenge we face to help, encourage, and reinforce comrades whose oppression in capitalist society—and sometimes double or triple oppression—teaches them day in and day out that they are *not* leaders. That is why we pay special attention, and act affirmatively in our branches to give an extra push, to potential leaders from the ranks of the oppressed. Any revolutionary party that doesn't do that is defaulting on its responsibilities.

This is not a moral question, as it is often posed by liberals. It is an objective necessity that flows from the kind of proletarian leadership required today to assure the victory of the workers' and farmers' struggle for power in this country and on a world scale.

Our perspective and norms on affirmative action are counterposed to two alternative roads that are generally destructive in a revolutionary working-class organization.

One is the quota system. We are opposed to quotas in the election of the leadership of our party today—at the same time that we are intransigent on why there *must* be quotas to make affirmative action programs real in virtually every other organization in capitalist society, governmental or otherwise. We generally support quotas in other organizations we belong to that don't have our communist program and organizational norms.

The 1978 NC report on "Leading the Party Into Industry" took up the reasons for this:

> Affirmative action is a fake in industry, in education, without quotas. Quotas are the only possible way we can check the rulers, can force them to retreat. It's the only way that we can raise people's consciousness about this.
>
> Quotas are necessary in another arena too. Quotas are needed in the workers' movement. For instance, in various situations in the unions today. Why must we have affirmative-action quotas in the unions? Why must we fight for the establishment of women's committees, for the right of all-Black caucuses and all-women's caucuses to function in the union? We do it because of the program of the union bureaucracy. It is not a program in the interest of the class. The leadership of the unions is not democratically elected to carry out a program in the interests of the class. One of the ways we can bust this down and change this is by fighting for quotas . . .

But we do not use the same criteria within the Leninist party. We must remember the differences. The party's program is a revolutionary program. The party's leadership is democratically elected. The only way the party can function is to base every decision on *political* criteria. And the only way to keep the real leadership (in the eyes of the party) and the elected leadership the same is to function in this way. The party is the *conscious* vanguard of the class. These are the decisive elements that make the party different from the unions today, from the other mass organizations of the class, from the future soviets. Remember, we don't advocate all our Leninist organizational norms for any other organization.

So we are against quotas, against caucuses in the Leninist party. But we are for affirmative action in leadership development and advancement. We are for finding ways and means on all levels to advance party leadership experience of comrades of oppressed nationalities, women comrades, young workers. We are for maximizing the pace of that experience, and maximizing the formal decisions that reflect and encourage that experience. [See excerpt from "Leading the Party into Industry," elsewhere in this issue.]

We are also opposed to the informal, de facto quotas that you find in organizations such as the Communist Party. It's inconceivable that a Communist Party convention would elect a new National Council with a smaller percentage of Blacks than the outgoing council. It's part of the CP's whole bureaucratic structure. The facade versus the real leadership, the top-down designation of leaders instead of their democratic selection by the ranks. It's a fake. That's not to say that there are no leaders of the CP who are Black. There certainly are, but when the formal leadership bodies of a communist party are not composed of the real leaders thrown up by the party in the course of the class struggle experiences they are living through, then the entire structure is a bureaucratic fraud, riddled with paternalism and corruption.

If we reject replacing affirmative action in the party by quotas, we also reject replacing it with the myth that there are and should be no special categories. The pretense that leadership selection can be color blind and sex blind is equally destructive to the fiber and morale of a revolutionary party. "We simply elect people on their merits." Whenever you hear that, you know that some other game is being run. That's not the way this society works, and we all know it. Or, "If all other factors are equal, we would choose the individual who is female, or Black." Those kinds of statements are always a cover-up for institutionalizing prejudice, protecting individuals who *can't* stand on their merits if other factors are equal.

All of these are aspects of leadership development that we have dealt with numerous times in the recent years. But we have to go back and review them periodically, because they are the fundamentals for us. They are the starting point for thinking out the question—"What is the National Committee?"—and preparing the election of the NC. Our capacity to be objective in discussing, acting, and leading on these kinds of questions is the reason we have continued to move forward in the real development of leadership cadres from the exploited and oppressed classes and from other oppressed layers of capitalist society.

This is registered in the leadership of the party today. But it is not something we can ever take for granted. It must be continuously reconquered in consciousness and in practice.

A fifteen-year perspective

It is useful to take a look at the evolution of the National Committee over the last decade and a half and think about the leadership challenges that have shaped it. The election of the National Committee at each convention is an eminently political action, and the leadership questions facing the delegates are not static. They evolve as the party itself changes from year to year and as the class struggle poses new challenges to which the party responds.

Following the 1971 convention Farrell Dobbs, who was then the national secretary, prepared a "Memorandum on the Leadership Question" that began with the summary statement: "Little progress was made at the last party convention in carrying forward the necessary transitions in leadership."

That was precisely the challenge facing the party in 1971. For almost a decade we had been recruiting steadily among the youth who were radicalizing in response to the mass civil rights movement, the Cuban revolution, and in opposition to the war in Vietnam. By 1970, the pace of that recruitment had begun to accelerate significantly. A new generation of cadres was coming forward, taking on an increasing burden of the day-to-day responsibilities—in the mass movement and the party apparatus as well. But there was a growing gap between this reality and the composition of the National Committee.

In his usual pedagogical manner, Farrell noted that of the 28 regular members of the outgoing committee, 27 had stood for reelection and been returned to the committee. Thus only one new comrade had been incorporated as a regular member. Five of the alternates elected were new to the committee, but even this had been accomplished by not reelecting four relatively young comrades who had previously served on the NC. The ranking of alternates shifted somewhat, with younger comrades moving up and older comrades down.

That, Farrell noted, did not add up to an adequate pace of transition, and it was up to the National Committee to take the lead in advancing this process more rapidly.

It's interesting to note, for the purposes of comparison later on, that of the National Committee elected in 1971 only 17 percent were women, although the party was 37 percent female. It took a number of years for the rise of the feminist movement and the accelerated recruitment of women to be registered in the National Committee. Seven percent of the National Committee (and four-and-a-half percent of the party) were comrades who were Black. One percent of the members and five percent of the National Committee were Latino.

In the early 1970s the task of organizing and assuring the transition in leadership was our central challenge. It posed some problems that were unique in the history of the revolutionary workers' movement, and we succeeded in meeting them.

We avoided the destructiveness of a "youth revolt" that would have eroded our foundations, warped our continuity, and profoundly miseducated the young cadres on all questions of leadership. That is what happened in a number of sections of the Fourth International. This is one of the things Farrell was always good on. He understood better than anyone the strengths and weaknesses of the party leadership, and he more than anyone was decisive in leading the older generations of cadres to make the difficult transition of relinquishing day-to-day political and organizational responsibility as younger comrades proved capable of taking it on. None of the older cadres ever doubted where Farrell stood on that or were willing to challenge his lead.

At the same time, however, Farrell always made it clear that he would fight—and there is no doubt we would have defeated—any "young turks rebellion." He was determined to *lead* a transition, so that the rope of continuity we talked about earlier would not be severed, with all the negative consequences that would have had for the party.

Because of the strengths of the party leadership, we made it through the decade of the 1970s and into the 1980s before any section of older cadres tried to claim the mantle of age to justify refusal to be disciplined unless the majority did things their way, supposedly the "old way."

It's important to bear in mind that the split that came to a head in 1982–83 was, in part, a split we had prevented year after year throughout the 1970s as we made the transition in leadership and carried out the turn. As the final section of the political resolution explains, the turn to the industrial unions and our orientation to the revolutionary leaderships in Central America and the Caribbean are steps toward building the kind of party that we set out to construct from our founding more than half a century ago—a party that is a living organism, not an ossified sect, responding to and advancing with our class on a world scale. We split with a layer of comrades who did not feel at home, or no longer felt at home, in that kind of proletarian party.

Farrell always used to insist that when the party was finally able to begin to break out of the semisectarian existence imposed on us by our forced isolation from the labor movement, many of the cadres who would find it hardest to orient themselves politically in the working-class struggles of the 1980s would be those whose concept of union work derived from their experiences in the unions in the 1940s and 1950s. Some would become an obstacle to reknitting our communist continuity back through the Teamsters battles of the 1930s, and to relearning how a party of worker-Bolsheviks acts to lead the vanguard of our class.

But the transition in the early and mid-1970s and the turn at the end of that decade were accomplished without a split within the political cadre that had led the party for decades. Nor was there any split along generational lines. When some individuals who left the party last year tried to turn it into an "old timers" revolt, it was too late. The split that Farrell always knew was inevitable could no longer damage the party, because we had *made* the transition in leadership. We had carried through the turn before the split developed. The "old timers" scam proved a fiasco, as the older cadres themselves divided and the bulk of the comrades over 50 remained with the party either as members or sympathizers.

A period of rapid change

The 1971 memorandum prepared by Farrell, the reports and discussion in the National Committee, and other leadership moves had an impact. The 1973 convention made some progress, incorporating five new regular members and 13 new alternate members on the National Committee.

In 1975, the convention took a bigger step. The National Committee recommended and the delegates concurred with the proposal to eliminate the category of advisory members of the National Committee. Advisory membership had been established in 1963 in order to open up room on the regular National Committee as the generation of Jim Cannon and Ray Dunne and a few other longtime party leaders who were regular members of the NC retired from day-to-day national leadership responsibilities.

It proved a useful vehicle for a period, but in 1975 the Political Committee recommended that the time had come to end it, and the National Committee unanimously concurred. A permanent "upper house" of the National Committee, composed of members with few responsibilities but all the rights of NC members, was not a desirable institution. It was a temporary measure to meet an extraordinary situation. It had accomplished its purpose and should be ended.

None of the nine advisory members in 1975

stood for election as regular members, and the convention decided to expand the number of regular and alternate National Committee members by ten. The alternate list was used to bring on 14 comrades who were not on the previous NC. The Nominations Commission report to the convention that year quoted from a 1946 letter of Cannon's, and noted that it had been guided by his admonition that the NC should not be a body from which members are removed only with a chisel. It should not be unusual, the Nominations Commission noted, for a comrade to be elected as an alternate member of the NC, to serve in that capacity for several years, to go off the NC for a period, and then perhaps be reelected at a subsequent convention.

In 1975, 1976, and 1977 we had three conventions in a row, each of which expanded the size of the National Committee. That was the period of the most rapid growth of the party, topping out at roughly 1,700 members and provisional members near the end of 1977.

In 1976 the delegates expanded the number of regular members of the NC by three. The committee elected that year registered the leadership development that had taken place among the young cadres who had not only demonstrated branch leadership, but were also veterans of the national leadership of the Boston desegregation struggle and the building of the National Student Coalition Against Racism.

The 1977 convention decided on a further substantial expansion of the National Committee. The Nominations Commission, following the general lead given by the National Committee, proposed an expansion of sixteen; and then the convention delegates, after some discussion, decided to add another five alternates.

The discussion on the election of the National Committee at that convention, however, as we noted in the report adopted in 1978, was so seriously off base politically that it was a warning sign. It alerted us to the need to clarify our leadership norms and criteria, have a thorough leadership discussion, and confront the pressures we were coming under.

The 1977 convention debate headed down two false tracks. On one hand the argument was advanced that there were too many "white males" in the leadership, and that was a problem for the party. It was suggested that the National Committee could be improved by taking off any white male and putting a woman nominee on. The party supposedly had too many leaders to fit on the National Committee, so "white males" should be limited. In the process of sweeping aside the category, a good many comrades carrying major leadership responsibilities in the branches were eliminated from serious and objective consideration for the National Committee, which weakened rather than strengthened its authority.

Secondly, there was an underlying assumption running through the 1977 convention deliberations that electing somebody to the National Committee was the way to make her or him a leader. That is, if we put more comrades who are Black or female on the NC, we will then have more leaders who are Black or female; instead of, if the party succeeds in helping more comrades who are workers or Black or female to move forward as leaders, that fact will then be registered in the election of the National Committee. We were drifting toward having quotas for oppressed nationalities and women on the National Committee under the pretense that this was the way to develop leadership, rather than recognizing that such a course would represent an evasion of our responsibilities.

Another interrelated problem surfaced at the 1977 convention—a "third-world-comrades-only" social was organized one evening there. It was not an event scheduled by the convention. To the contrary, other social activities organized by the convention were taking place at the same time. But the fact of the party was spread by word of mouth. Comrades arriving with companions who were not Black or Latino were told that these convention participants could not come in. International guests of the convention who were of European descent were asked to leave.

As soon as the convention presiding committee learned of this exclusive social gathering, a special point was added to the agenda to discuss the implications of such a thing occurring at a communist convention. The delegates adopted a report explaining why party social events that exclude some comrades on the basis of sex, nationality, race, or language are contrary to Leninist organizational norms. Pointing to the parallel with women's caucuses or gay caucuses, which are by definition constituted on a basis other than *political* criteria, the report explained that such activities organized under the guise of being social gatherings foster cliquism, and are destructive to the party's capacity to cut across the race, sex, age, nationality, language, and other divisions within the working class and forge a politically homogeneous cadre through common experience in struggle. [See "Leninist Norms and Nonexclusive Party Social Affairs," by Catarino Garza, report adopted by SWP National Convention, 1977, printed elsewhere in this bulletin.]

These two discussions, on leadership criteria and on other norms, were interrelated. Disturbing as they were, they were a pale reflection of the destructive battles over these questions taking place in a number of other sections of the Fourth International, to say nothing of other organizations on the left. They registered the political and social pressures the party was under.

These debates burst into the open at the 1977 convention because we had not prepared adequately. The National Committee had not given the necessary leadership in advance of the convention. It was a salutary lesson, and we set out to correct that error in the period between the 1977 and 1979 conventions.

At the beginning of 1978 we decided to organize the turn to industry and rapidly began to build several industrial fractions. As part of the turn report we began to discuss all these questions of leadership norms and criteria. We prepared the leadership school and launched its first session in March 1980. We helped lead the fight on each of these questions throughout the International. All this was registered in the character of the discussion at the 1979 convention, the reports on the turn and women's liberation adopted by the 1979 World Congress, and in our capacity to consolidate our gains and deepen our understanding of the leadership questions facing the party.

By the 1981 convention, we again faced a new challenge: bringing onto the National Committee a layer of comrades who had actually led the turn and proved their capacities to lead the party in action. A significant change in the composition of the NC was needed for it to reflect the real experiences of our cadres in the industrial working class and in the union fractions through which the party was being built. The delegates elected a National Committee that included 16 comrades as regular members and 25 as alternates who had not been on the outgoing committee.

Finally, last year, in 1984, as we discussed, the overriding responsibility of the convention was to reduce the size of the NC to make it a workable committee and to bring it into balance with the party. We accomplished that and are now ready to move forward along the lines of the proposals we made at the beginning of the report.

Two other points should be noted, however, concerning the last NC election. As Rashaad [Ali] indicated in the report from the Nominations Commission to the delegates last year, there was one big change between 1981 and 1984. The Nominations Commission found that it was not necessary to give special consideration to comrades leading our industrial union fractions. Leadership there overlapped with other leadership responsibilities to such a large degree, that the commission felt no special measures were necessary. That's a tribute to the success of the turn.

Secondly, the percentage of women on the National Committee went down from 37 to 32 percent. In and of itself, that fact is not a cause for concern. The percentage of comrades on the National Committee who are workers, or Black, or women, or Puerto Rican, or Asian, or Chicano is naturally going to fluctuate from one year to the next. It's inevitable because the class-struggle experiences we live through—both their pace and character—have a powerful impact on our recruitment, on the development of leadership, and on the rate of attrition. That can't help but be registered in changes in our leading bodies. What would be cause for concern is if such percentages didn't change; or if the proportion of comrades who are Black or female always went up but never down; or always down but never up. That would indicate there was something artificial in the way we were selecting our leadership, that we were not being ruthlessly objective with ourselves.

The offensive against women's rights

When we see changes of that character, however, we owe it to ourselves to take a closer look and try to sort out the factors involved. So I want to take the rest of the report to deal with a broader economic and social question that does bear on our recruitment and leadership development: the character of the ruling-class offensive against women's rights and the impact this has had on even the most conscious layers of our class.

This is an important aspect of the pressures that are coming down on us as a small, vanguard proletarian party. The sustained campaign to take back some of the gains women have made is an important barometer of the kind of political period we're living through.

I want to start with one fact. For the first time in nearly 15 years, women constitute less than 40 percent of the party membership—39 percent to be precise, according to the last membership survey in October 1984. Following the rise of the feminist movement at the end of the 1960s and the significant recruitment to the party out of those struggles, the proportion of the party that was female remained remarkably stable throughout the 1970s and early 1980s. The percentage fluctuated between roughly 42 and 44 percent—both when we were growing rapidly and when we were losing slowly.

This was one of the statistics that we watched closely as the party got into industry, as well. We noted the importance of the fact that such a "wrenching turn" had no negative impact on the relative numbers of women in the party. To the contrary, women comrades from the beginning were proportionally represented in our industrial fractions.

So, when the number of women suddenly fell by several percentage points in a six-month time period in 1984, it was a significant development. It is a more important statistic than the decrease in the percentage of women on the National Committee at the last convention, although the two things are not unrelated.

Upon reflection, this should come as no surprise to us. It is another confirmation that we are correct in our political assessment of the character and weight of the ruling-class offensive against the gains of the women's movement. Women are targeted as part of the broad and many-sided assault on the rights and standard of living of the exploited producers, by means of which the owners of capital are trying to shift the relationship of class forces to their own advantage.

The attacks on women's rights are of a piece with the drive to cut wages and social services, lengthen hours, gut health and safety regulations, and increase the rate of exploitation through all the mechanisms at their disposal. The attacks on democratic rights, on affirmative action, desegregation, and other gains of the Black movement; the attempts to intimidate and terrorize undocumented workers; the intensification of anticommunist propaganda as part of the U.S.–organized war in Central America—all these are part of the same large tableau.

As always, however, whenever the ruling class has the bit in its teeth, whenever the bosses are on a stepped-up *offensive* to shift the relationship of class forces in their direction—as they have been for the last decade—women are and must be a special target. It's not just working-class women who find themselves in the line of fire, however. It is women, the second sex.

This attack on women and their rights is fundamental to the success of the capitalist offensive, because it is one of the important ways in which the rulers work to deepen the divisions within the working class. The purpose is to change the way women think of themselves; to weaken and undercut their *class* consciousness as workers; to heighten their consciousness of themselves as women—and not in the feminist sense. The bosses' slogan is "let women be women, and contented with their lot." It's not "let women be workers and lead their sisters forward."

But the goal of the offensive on women's rights is not to drive women out of industry. It never has been—any more than *la migra* is trying to prevent undocumented workers from getting employment. One proof of this is that the percentage of the work force that is female has been rising, from one plateau to another, ever since the beginning of the industrial revolution. The bosses' aim is rather to make women more vulnerable to increased exploitation. It is not to push them out of the labor market altogether, but to push them down.

In a period such as this, the owners of capital need an expanded pool of unemployed workers, an industrial reserve army of labor, reconstituted on an enlarged base. Women have always been an important component. The ideological campaign aimed at women serves to reinforce their tendency to view themselves as only marginal workers, as temporary workers, as a "second" wage earner in the family. Women are supposed to accept unemployment with less resistance and resentment, because they "normally" aren't meant to be working anyway. Aren't their children being permanently damaged by abandonment in childcare facilities, or turning into lonely latch-key delinquents? In periods of rising unemployment, there are always assertions by ruling class "opinion molders" that the statistics are *artificially* high because they include so many women; everyone knows they really shouldn't be counted as unemployed in the same way as men.

The goal is to force women to internalize their dependency, to cause them to blame themselves, not the social relations of production. Rather than demanding as a *right* access to higher-paying jobs in occupations previously closed to them, women are pushed toward being grateful for any job. At any wage.

Part of the strategy is also to break ties and intensify competition between white women and Black women, as well as between women who are fighting their way into nontraditional jobs and Blacks, who constitute a disproportionately large number of the more conscious, vanguard layers of the working class.

The accelerated increase in the numbers of working women, beginning in the early 1960s, was followed by the "second wave" of the women's movement during the late 1960s and early 1970s. Because of the strength of these advances and the broad changes of consciousness that came with them, the counteroffensive against women's rights in the last few years has been all the more concerted. It has taken numerous forms.

- The defeat of the Equal Rights Amendment.
- The onslaught against abortion rights—from the withholding of funds to the bombing of clinics. Day in and day out, the propaganda that abortion is murder, murder, murder.
- The glorification of the family, built around women's special fulfillment of themselves as mothers. Supermom is in. She works a full-time job. OK, she's got a right to work. But when she comes home she really makes sure her kids—and husband—don't suffer too much for her selfish absorption in her own life. And, deep down, she really has a lot of doubts about whether she's doing the right thing. Isn't this "new woman" wonderful? How many guilt-tripping articles have you seen like that in the last couple of years?
- The concerted drive to roll back affirmative action gains, to foster the "white-male" backlash against Blacks and women. The goal is not to push women out of the few niches they have secured in job areas previously closed to them, whether it's the mines or the steel mills. It is to deepen divisions and competition, heighten insecurity, promote the idea that women don't really have the right to be there. Since they're taking jobs men ought to have, women are responsible for the high rate of unemployment of Black males, especially.

The counteroffensive to roll back women's confidence and combativity has been registered in the decline of the women's movement. The thousands of small circles of feminist activists have disappeared. The few groups that have survived largely concentrate on specific interests such as health or art. Others have been drawn into reactionary campaigns demanding more cops as an answer to the problem of rape, or calling for censorship laws as the way to deal with pornography. Since 1977 the National Organization for Women has been gutted, turned largely into an electoralist appendage of the capitalist two-party system.

The last time a sizeable women's rights action occurred in this country was 1978—seven years ago. That was the July 9, 1978, March on Washington called by NOW to demand an extension of the deadline for ratification of the ERA. There's been no significant women's liberation action since then, despite the potential that existed around the ERA, especially.

There is no mass fighting women's movement in the streets or anywhere else today. We don't have the kind of movement from which women gain confidence as they fight for their rights, fight to change things that vitally affect their lives. The kind of mass women's movement through which women can, from their own experiences, learn the fundamental lessons of class struggle and proletarian leadership. That doesn't exist today. The women's liberation forces are on the defensive, not the offensive.

This situation is not unique to the United States.

It is a general phenomenon that, to varying degrees, marks virtually all the advanced capitalist countries where the women's movement had a significant impact in the 1970s. The reasons for the decline of the women's movement are also fundamentally the same elsewhere, rooted in the beginning of the capitalist austerity drive in the 1974–75 recession, and the incapacity of the current officialdom of the labor movement to mount any effective fightback. Once again it was proven that the fate of the women's liberation movement is not independent of the historic course of the working class, even if it can on occasion surge ahead and help show the way forward.

This is one reason why the abortion rights struggle taking place in Canada right now is important. It's an exception to the general picture. The size and strength and militancy of the demonstrations that have been organized are an inspiration to women everywhere who want to fight, and we should take full advantage of that to educate women in the United States, as well. When our *Militant* reporter recently returned from Toronto and Montréal where she went to do some stories, her first remark was, "I'd forgotten what it was like."

It's been so many years since we've been part of a movement that organized actions of thousands of chanting, singing, fighting, enthusiastic women who felt strong and confident that we *do* forget what it is like. And that is one of the things that is weighing on us today. We are feeling the impact of what is *not* happening as well as what is, and how that affects even the most conscious women.

Pressures in industry are fewer

Women who are full-time industrial workers and part of the union movement are in the best position to resist the conservatizing pressures that all women are subjected to by this economic and political offensive of the ruling class. These women—among whom are most of the women who are members of our movement—have a greater degree of confidence that comes from knowing that they can sell their labor power and survive, thus being able to have some small element of independence in making important decisions affecting their lives. They have acquired at least the beginning of class consciousness through understanding that they have a better chance at improving wages and working conditions by joining together with fellow workers to fight the employer. Moreover, despite the bosses' attempts to foster animosity, women in industry are frequently working alongside male co-workers in job situations where each depends on the other and relations of mutual confidence can develop.

In addition to all these factors, women who are communists are also politically conscious—as workers and as women—and have the advantage of being part of an organized vanguard party that politically orients itself and collectively carries out its work. So party members are in the best position of all to stand up to the pressures on women today.

That does not mean we escape them, however, and we confront them even in industry. We're part of our class, and the offensive on women's rights is aimed at our class above all. We are constantly fighting the suggestions that we're not really workers; that it is a temporary condition; that the important thing is we are women; that women are only a marginal part of the working class; that we are not hereditary proletarians; that we work for a while and then we leave the work force to raise a family; that we work part time or on and off, switching jobs. We're constantly being told that what really defines our lives is not selling our labor power, but home and husband and children.

Because we work with men and women who are generally more influenced than we are by the attitudes and assumptions fostered by the rulers' pervasive propaganda, the truth is that we find it harder today than we did five years ago to simply be ourselves with our coworkers. It's harder to simply be the kind of women (and men) we are: women who are class conscious, political, workers. Communists. Women whose being is not defined by children and family. Women whose interests are focused on being active builders of the revolutionary workers' movement, from which we derive great satisfaction. That's who we are.

We feel more pressure today, from family and coworkers both, to adapt to conservative attitudes and the backward expectations put forward as the norm by the ruling-class propaganda. We put on wedding rings. We make up stories about kids we don't have. We do all kinds of things.

What we are trying to sort out here is not the

element of these kinds of pressures that always surround us, but what has changed over the last five years. That is what is important. And comrades generally feel more on the defensive today in explaining why they *don't* have any children, for example, or why they're *not* married to someone they're living with.

In part this is because party members are, on the average, older, so our friends and associates on the job tend to be older too, and more likely to be married and have families themselves. But it's not only that. Many comrades have had the experience of wondering how best to respond when an acquaintance on the job asks, in a friendly way, if you're married or how many children you have. When it's a discussion between women you often sense that if you say, "No, I'm not married," or "No, I don't have any kids," then you will also have to add something by way of explanation—because the question marks will be all over the other person's face, even if she thinks it's impolite to ask, "Why not?"

When it's appropriate to do so, such questions can immediately get you into a political discussion, as you talk about what you're interested in and what you do with your time when you're not working. But sometimes you just have to try to avoid the discussion.

One thing that we should be clear about is that the pressures women comrades are more aware of today do not come from the turn. We aren't *more* susceptible to the ideological counteroffensive of the ruling class because we are more working class in social composition and milieu. Just the opposite. That's obvious if you stop and consider what kinds of political and social pressures are registered by the "yuppie" phenomenon. If our membership and milieu were primarily middle-class, middle-aged radical and ex-radical professionals and white collar workers, we know what kinds of conservative, despairing conclusions we would be adapting to.

We should also correct another error we have sometimes made in trying to sort out the difficulties facing women comrades in industry. Sexual harassment is a real thing that women have always had to deal with on the job. And it increases in periods like today when the bosses are on the prod. It is one of the issues our fractions need to be constantly alert to, striving to advance consciousness and to win the unions to effectively combat. The reason comrades get hassled and targeted for sexual harassment, however, is first and foremost because we're communists. The bosses want us to quit the party, to quit being leaders. The fact that we are women, of course, gives them an additional way to try to turn the screws on us. But the biggest pressure on the job comes from being a worker-Bolshevik. That is what's difficult. Being a woman in industry is not nearly so hard.

The clearest proof of this is that so few women comrades who leave the party pointing to the pressures of working in industry actually end up quitting their jobs. They quit being communists, and then they find that it's really not so hard to be a worker.

Impact on party

Even though women in the party are more conscious than anyone else about the ruling-class offensive and the ways in which women are singled out as a special target, and even though we're more capable of being objective about the pressures we're under as a small working class–vanguard party, we don't live in an isolation ward. The economic, social, and political conditions that surround us bear down harder on women in the party than on men. That is a fact.

There is another element involved, too, and that is age. The median age of the entire party has gone up, and that means the median age of women in the party has also risen. It is a simple fact of life in class society that aging takes a bigger toll on women than on men. Women are taught by all their life experiences, by all the ways they are molded and conditioned in this society, that it is all over by the time you hit 40. You're over the hill. You're no longer of any interest to men. And if you've got a man, you better hold on to him, because you won't get another one.

You're too old to reproduce, so you have no use value anymore. That's another theme we've seen article after article over the last few years—the dangers of having children too late in life. They are aimed at women in their 20s and 30s, and the message is clear. You better have that kid now. If you don't, you'll be sorry, because the likelihood is that any child you give birth to a few years from now will be retarded or deformed. And it will be your fault, because you selfishly wanted to postpone having children until you were too old to produce a healthy baby.

All of this has its impact on women as political beings, and on women as leaders. We've discussed before why women tend to pull back from leadership responsibility, especially from trying to lead men, because they know that few men can tolerate the challenge of women like that. Girls learn early on in life that being a leader will have all kinds of repercussions on personal relationships with men. But the fear of leading, the self-limitation, increases as women get older. It's not always a conscious decision. But the fear of being alone takes on greater weight.

That is why you usually have a higher percentage of women in the leadership of a youth organization than in the party. When you're 18 or 20 you're really not worried about being lonely when you get to be 50 or 60. That's simply a fact. A positive one. You're less inclined to make personal compromises and limit yourself in order to please someone else. You don't put so much store on planning what you hope will be a "permanent" relationship.

These more general kinds of pressure on women in the party are always with us to some degree. But they are exacerbated by the slow advance of the working-class movement and the slow pace of recruitment today. Women aren't carried along by a rising movement. The difficulties seem greater, the solutions fewer, the struggle more protracted.

All these things combined are why we see a small decline in the percentage of women in the party, and why it should come as no surprise.

Given the scope of the changes over the last 40 years in the economic and social conditions women face, it is unlikely that the decline will be large or long-lasting. Women will be centrally involved in every aspect of struggle as working people find the road to effective fightback. This will lead to new recruitment and new leaders coming forward, as well as a new upsurge of the women's movement. But that's not happening yet.

Some parallels with the '50s

In thinking about the conditions we are facing today, it's useful to go back to some of the experiences that the party went through in the period of post–World War II reaction. The overwhelming majority of our members today did not live through those years as conscious political people. Some weren't even born yet. But a better knowledge of the party in this period of our history helps to put some of our experience today in perspective.

The 1980s is not the same as the 1950s, of course. This is not the place to review all the similarities and differences. We've done that in other reports and in the political resolutions we adopted at our last convention.

For the purposes of the questions we're dealing with here, however, we should note that while the ruling class is on the offensive, the political reaction is not so deep. The whole world context is different. Moreover, the changes brought about by the accelerated integration of women into the labor force in the postwar period, and the subsequent rise of the women's liberation movement, have substantially altered the economic and political context from that of the late 1940s and early 1950s.

Some of the things that we are experiencing today, however, are neither new nor mysterious. It's a real political education to go back and look at the ways in which the postwar "feminine mystique" offensive affected the party itself.

One useful thing we can do is to make accessible to comrades today the chapter of party history known as "the Bustelo controversy." The only small piece of the record that most comrades may have read is an article by Evelyn Reed printed in her book, *Problems of Women's Liberation*. It's called, "Cosmetics, Fashions and the Exploitation of Women." That piece is actually an excerpt from a contribution to the SWP Discussion Bulletin written in 1954 and entitled, "The Woman Question and the Marxist Method."

The introduction to the article comments that many of the issues being raised by the women's movement in the late 1960s are not new. It goes on to note that a discussion on the question of cosmetics and fashion took place in the Socialist Workers Party in the early 1950s, and identifies Reed's article as part of that debate. That offers only a hint of the reality, to say the least.

When a sharp division over cosmetics and fashions broke out in the party in the early 1950s, it was not an academic sociological debate. Nor was it a frivolous diversion, despite the fact that it hardly seems to be a question of world historic importance. To the contrary, it was related to the most profound questions of maintaining a proletarian party under conditions of reaction. It would be hard to find a more instructive example of the way reactionary ruling-class propaganda finds an expression within the workers' vanguard, especially when it's under pressure. And the pedagogical way the party sought to bring out the underlying issues is also an education in leadership methods, so it's worth taking time for a short digression to sketch the basic elements.

In 1954 the Cold War and anticommunist witch-hunt still dominated all political life in the United States. The party had just suffered one of the deepest splits in its history, the Cochran split, which cut through the basic leadership cadre, taking a quarter of the National Committee and some 20 percent of the membership.

In July of 1954, a *Militant* staff writer using the pen name Jack Bustelo—whose style many of you will find familiar if you've read much of Joe Hansen—wrote an article called, "Sagging Cosmetic Lines Try a Face Lift." It is a wonderful example of a short, agitational piece of basic socialist education. The article begins by noting how a recession that had just begun was cutting into the cosmetics industry's profits, because women who were unemployed were buying fewer cosmetics. The merchants of beauty had announced their plans to revive profits by convincing women to buy more cosmetics again.

Bustelo wrote: "The Toilets Goods Association reports that after 13 years of steady gains, cosmetics manufacturers' sales suddenly plunged in the first quarter of 1954—right when unemployment took a steep jump." In response, he explained, the big cosmetics dealers were projecting "Operation Big Push." "Toni, for example, has announced its third new cosmetic in three months, a face cream that no words can describe except Deep Magic."

Bustelo then went on to explain what we all know: how the cosmetics industry plays on women's insecurities and fears to try to make us buy cosmetics.

The letters of outrage and indignation began arriving on the *Militant* editor's desk in a matter of days. I doubt that Bustelo was surprised. He probably wrote the article precisely because he knew what kind of reactionary pressures were finding echoes within the party, and his aim was true.

For several weeks the debate took place in the pages of the *Militant*, with letters to the editor and a reply from Bustelo. One reader objected that Bustelo's article was offensive because "one gets the feeling that it is women who are being made fun of." All women really want is "some loveliness and beauty in their lives," the reader argued, but "beauty is predominately monopolized by the wealthy."

"The wealthy are beautiful because the workers are wretched," this reader continued. Moreover, the fact that working-class women strive for beauty "has a progressive aspect, because it is part of the rebellion of women against a position which denies to them part of their rights as human beings."

Bustelo replied with a fine, short essay on beauty, class society, and historical materialism. "I do not believe," he wrote, "that 'beauty is predominantly monopolized by the wealthy,' and that the 'wealthy are beautiful because the workers are wretched.'

"It appears to me that you might just as well say that 'morality is predominantly monopolized by the wealthy,' and that the 'wealthy are moral because the workers are immoral.'" The norms of beauty, Bustelo pointed out, like the norms of morals, are determined in the final analysis by the ruling class. And, he added, "I think most of the customs and norms of capitalist society are ridiculous and even vicious, including the customs and norms of wealthy bourgeois women."

To express that view is hardly making fun of women.

Bustelo's reply provoked further outraged responses. Several readers wrote in defending the use of cosmetics as a basic economic necessity for working women to get a job and keep a man. They argued that the party should defend woman's "right" to use cosmetics.

The last letter printed in the *Militant* accused Bustelo of "third period" Stalinist sectarianism, because, according to the reader, Bustelo advocated "the concept that a woman should be satisfied with ill fitting, poor quality clothing, or that her hair and makeup do not matter because there are more important things." That, said the reader, is the same thing the bourgeoisie tries to convince workers of so they won't demand the same products that the rulers consume.

"Of course," the reader argued, "these standards are bourgeois standards, but they are the norms the women have to meet. . . . If the women want these things, they should have them, and we have to support them in their struggle to get them. . . . It is part of the struggle of women to emancipate themselves from the status of household drudges and to acquire an individuality of their own."

As the character of the divisions became clearer, the Political Committee made a decision to take the debate out of the pages of the *Militant* and to continue it internally. In October 1954 a *Discussion Bulletin* was published containing the letters and critical articles that were not printed in the *Militant,* along with major replies by Evelyn Reed and Jack Bustelo. The full scope of the reactionary pressures coming in on the party are even clearer in this internal bulletin.

A comrade by the name of Marjorie McGowan, a member of the Los Angeles branch, said it all most clearly. She left the party very soon after she wrote her contributions printed in the internal bulletin, and you can certainly see some of the reasons why. McGowan's letter begins by extolling "the revolution in technology and science," which, according to her, had "reached its highest development under capitalism in the last 40 years" and had "wrought a partial revolution in all phases of life."

A revolution has occurred, she argues, "in the relation between the sexes, in sexual morality, in medicine, in nutrition and health, in architecture, in art, in beauty, in hobbies for leisure, in city-planning, in child-rearing, in methods of education, in psychology." This is written from Los Angeles, remember, in 1954.

"These new, progressive and highly creative developments in all phases of life," she continues for the record, can only be finally realized by socialism. In the meantime, of course, "revolution" is changing everything for the better. This is the context for the discussion on cosmetics, because, "What holds true for the rest of life also relates to beauty in the female form."

The revolutionary changes "in the standards of beauty," McGowan states, "flow out of and parallel the concurrent revolution in sexual morality of the last 35 years or so. The long-stemmed American beauty," she raves on, "full of natural vitality and physical grace, with shining hair, clear eyes, smooth skin and natural cosmetics with a trace of accent here and there, is no fiction but an American commonplace. This type of beauty is the American social standard."

It is "an inherent part of every normal female ego to strive toward the preservation" of this kind of beauty, and "this is a proper female goal worthy of the considered attention of a revolutionist."

In case you haven't yet figured out what class McGowan looks to lead the revolution she's interested in, she eliminates all ambiguities: "There is nothing beautiful in the dishpan hands, the premature wrinkles, the scraggly hair, the dumpy figures in the dumpy housedresses, the ugly furniture and the hodge-podge accessories of the working-class woman and her home."

Not surprisingly, McGowan's espousal of the U.S. imperialist bourgeoisie's racist standards of "beauty," and her contempt for the working class, were accompanied by an open rejection of the historical discoveries of materialists that enabled us for the first time to understand the origin of women's oppression. The Spring 1954 issue of the party's magazine the *Fourth International* had published an article by Evelyn Reed entitled "The Myth of Women's Inferiority," (which is available in *Problems of Women's Liberation*). This was followed by the publication of her "Sex and Labor in Primitive Society" in the Summer 1954 issue of the magazine. Both articles explain that human society has evolved through definite stages of economic and social development and that primitive communism, which was matriarchal in kinship-structure, came first in this historical sequence.

McGowan submitted a long article attempting to refute Reed. She demanded that the editors of the magazine and the party leadership repudiate the views expressed by Reed, which McGowan said were "scholastically irresponsible" and made the party "look ridiculous in the eyes of informed individuals in the bourgeois academic world."

McGowan made it clear that she knew her argument was with Marx and Engels, not just with Reed. She stated her "firm inner conviction that such interpretations of primitive society and primitive social forms as are current in the party today, and have been for the last 75 years or so, are not just accidentally false or innocently misguided."

As Reed noted in her reply, there is "only one interpretation of primitive society which has been current in the party for the last 75 years or so, and which, indeed, we have openly embraced. This is the *Marxist* interpretation, as it was set down by Engels in his *Origin of the Family, Private Property and the State.*"

The Political Committee rejected McGowan's request that the magazine's editors dissociate themselves from Reed's position. "The Political Committee felt it unnecessary to take a position either for or against Comrade Reed's articles," Farrell Dobbs wrote in an October 13, 1954, letter to McGowan. "On such subjects the feeling was that considerable latitude is permissible as long as the author defends the materialist viewpoint, advocates and tries to apply the dialectic method and seeks to supply material of an educational character.... From this standpoint, the editors were entirely correct in publishing the Reed articles."

In addition to taking up the challenge from McGowan on historical materialism and the origins of women's oppression—a battle that Evelyn returned to repeatedly over the next 25 years, leaving us with a rich educational legacy that we could be making more use of today than we are— both Reed and Bustelo wrote major articles for the internal bulletin taking up the issue raised by the "cosmetics" debate.

Bustelo's article, entitled "The Fetish of Cosmetics," is a basic piece of Marxist education on capitalism and commodity fetishism, and explains the controversy in the context of economic and social conditions of post–World War II U.S. society. The author's sense of humor makes it all the more enjoyable to read.

Reed's reply also takes up the issues from a basic materialist standpoint: that norms of beauty, like humanity itself, are the historical and changing product of social labor, and cannot be dissociated from the development of the productive forces or from the class struggle.

Reed also deals with the context of the debate in the party, noting that the "past 14 years of war boom and prosperity have produced a conservatizing effect upon the working class which we describe as a 'bourgeoisification.' One of the forms this takes is the readiness of the workers to accept bourgeois opinions and propaganda as scientific truth and adapt themselves to it.

"Like the whole working class," Reed emphasized, "the party is under constant pressure and bombardment from this massive bourgeois propaganda machine." Some of the discussions taking place in the party indicate that "a certain amount of adaptation to bourgeois propaganda has arisen which, although probably unwitting, is a signal that should alert us to the danger."

That is what the cosmetics controversy clearly revealed. "When the comrades defend the *right* of women to use cosmetics, fashions, etc.," Reed stated, "without clearly distinguishing between such a right and the *capitalist social compulsion* to use them, they have fallen into the trap of bourgeois propaganda."

It is true, she went on, that "so long as capitalism prevails, we must abide by these cosmetic and fashion decrees.... We must give at least a token recognition of the harsh reality. But this does not mean that we must accept these edicts and compulsions complacently, or without protest. The workers in the plants are often obliged to accept speedups, pay cuts and attacks on their unions. But they always and invariably accept them under protest, under continuing struggle against them and in a constant movement to *oppose* their needs and will against their exploiters.

"The class struggle is a movement of *opposition, not adaptation,* and this holds true not only of the workers in the plants, but of the women as well."

Reed also noted a second danger signal that pointed to the pressures the party was under. An important part of the background to the cosmetics debate, Reed commented, was that "for some months an informal discussion has been going on among some comrades on the problem of 'male chauvinism' as it relates to the party. A few comrades have felt that the party itself is not free from this and that women comrades are seriously hindered and handicapped by it."

The Bustelo controversy and the party today

Three aspects of this chapter of party history are particularly instructive.

Even if the objective conditions today are not as difficult as they were in 1954, the ruling-class counteroffensive against women's rights has had an impact on the working class, on women, and on the party. To deny this would be simply closing our eyes to reality.

The division in the party in 1954 over the cosmetics question helps us to understand how pervasive the pressures of bourgeois society can be, and the variety of ways in which they affect even the most conscious vanguard of the working class. We have to be conscious and *objective* about the pressures we're under. We have to strive to separate out the different elements that enter into our personal decisions, and not try to find political justifications or rationalizations for things we do—from the make up we use, to the food we like, to the music we listen to, or whatever.

As Evelyn put it, so long as capitalism survives, so long as the bourgeoisie remains the ruling class, workers will always have to abide by and make some concessions to the economic and social conditions we are struggling to change. But even when we *adapt*, especially when we *adapt*—which we all do all the time—we have to be conscious that this is what we're doing, and not pretend we're advancing the working class along its historic line of march. You don't have to turn make up into something progressive, into a right as opposed to a social compulsion, just because you want to dye your hair so you look younger!

This is also relevant to the decision individual comrades make about whether or not to have children. Nothing could be a more purely personal decision influenced by all kinds of factors, conscious and unconscious. The party couldn't possibly have a political position on so personal a question. But for the same reasons, it's an error to try to find political rationalizations for whatever one decides. Having children is neither more nor less proletarian. It's common to all classes. All the party demands is that we each try to act with as much consciousness as possible, and that we not try to mold the party to serve our personal needs, but to build it as the proletarian vanguard we strive to make it.

If we ever stop being able to be objective about ourselves in relation to the party and our class, then we cease being a vanguard revolutionary organization.

It is useful to consider the "Bustelo controversy" from a second angle: the role of the party in helping all of us to think objectively and politically about the conditions that shape us personally. This is hard to do on our own. Each of us needs to be part of an organized, conscious vanguard party in order not to be just pulled along—adapting, not opposing.

Thirdly, Evelyn's reference to the "informal discussion" on problems of male chauvinism in the party is also important to note. Why did "the woman question," as it used to be called in the workers' movement, became an explosive issue in the party in the 1950s? Not because male chauvinist discrimination unfairly excluded women members from leadership, but because "the woman question" became the banner of the Weiss clique that played a destructive role throughout the real dog-days of the 1950s.

As the party was forced deeper into a semisectarian existence by the objective limitations of the period, as there were few opportunities to turn outward and orient toward intervening in the class struggle, the tendency inevitably developed to search for the source of our problems closer to home. Turning inward and feeding on yourself invariably accompanies periods of reaction. Cliquism, subjectivity, and petty factionalism are fostered by the political difficulties.

Coming out of the Cochran split, a clique in the party led by a member of the Political Committee, Murry Weiss, sought to expand its influence in the party leadership and reduce the weight of the team of comrades that included Farrell Dobbs, Morris Stein, Joe Hansen, George Novack, Tom Kerry, and others. The primary banner under which the Weissites organized to advance members of their grouping in the party—male and female—was a war on "male chauvinism." Comrades such as Myra Tanner Weiss, Clara Kaye, and Frances James were not recognized as central leaders of the party, they claimed, for one simple reason: the male chauvinism of the party leadership. Farrell was considered to suffer the most advanced case of the disease, but every member of the Political Committee—except Murry Weiss—was incurable. The only men on the National Committee given a clean bill of health were, of course, members of the clique.

The goal of the Weissites was not helping

women in general to gain leadership confidence, but to advance women—and men—who agreed with them about the character of the party leadership's fatal flaws, its "conservatism." Their campaign was often directed against other women in the party, especially, since the fact that most *women* in the party did not think that Myra Tanner Weiss was a political leader of the caliber her group pretended was a damaging refutation of their entire case.

More than anything, this was a petty-bourgeois clique that directed its attacks on working-class women in the party. Leaders such as Farrell did everything possible to encourage and help organize classes for working women—including working women with children. They, of course, were the party members who had the most difficulty finding time to study. The Weissites, on the other hand, were vicious toward any woman comrade who didn't subscribe to their view of the chauvinist nature of the party leadership. She was labeled "ignorant"—the greatest insult a petty-bourgeois intellectual can imagine—and considered a dupe of the male leaders.

The Weiss clique, of course, generated a counter-clique that also tried to make "the woman question" its banner. Throughout the late 1950s and into the 1960s there were small-scale wars over which women would be elected to the National Committee. There were rather open battles to try to knock one woman off, or get another one on, by bullet balloting, or clique-organized votes to move someone from tenth alternate to fifth, and so on. It was the kind of petty, subjective stuff that is the antithesis of proletarian concepts of leadership. Few things could be more destructive in the election of a leadership body.

But this was all part of the party's forced retreat from proletarian norms under the adverse conditions of the years of reaction and isolation. Comrades who lived through this know very well how destructive it was, and how frustrating it was to be unable to do anything about it until political conditions began to change. It was impossible during that period to have objective discussion in the party on questions of women's liberation.

The Weiss clique itself was destroyed by the recruitment and growth of the party and YSA starting in the early 1960s. Those who were inspired, not demoralized, by the progress and development of the party broke from the clique and turned their energies toward responding to the new openings. The more the party recruited, the more ground the clique lost, the more antiparty they became, and the more they simply withdrew into their private salons to discuss why the party was finished. Some of the Weissites just quit; most were eventually dropped from membership for non-payment of dues. But the legacy of the traumatic battles over "the woman question" hung on, right up to the late 1960s when the new wave of the feminist movement buried it.

The rise of the women's liberation movement brought the definitive confirmation that the party leadership had a correct, revolutionary proletarian line on women's oppression, and sought to encourage women comrades to develop their capacities to the fullest. There was not a moment's hesitation about the importance of that movement or the need to orient the party toward the fullest involvement in it. We were unique on the U.S. left in our response to the women's liberation movement. The Communist Party, the Maoists, the Trotskyist sects—everyone else considered it petty bourgeois, anti-male, anti-Black, and divisive of the working class. And, to begin with, that was the majority view in the leadership of the Fourth International as well. The SWP responded as a proletarian vanguard from the start.

The chapter of party history we've been talking about here—including the destructive way the Weiss clique abused women in the party and made accusations of male chauvinism their battle cry—was closed with the new rise of the women's movement. We can look at it objectively now and learn from it precisely because it *is* history. If we had a Weiss-type clique in the NC today that hoisted the banner of combating male chauvinism in order to rally people against the party and push their people onto the NC, it would be more difficult to see this period clearly and draw the lessons. The fact that the Weissites operated in the leadership of the party was what gave the clique more appeal and made it more destructive.

In retrospect, it's easy to see how the political conditions created fertile ground for the growth of cliquism. When the going is tough it's always easier to find a scapegoat close to home. The class enemy out there is a big target to set your sights on. It's easier to take on something more modest in size. If the real obstacle to the party moving forward is not the strength and power of capitalism but a handful of men in the party, "them" in the leadership who are mucking us over, who are always on our case, who don't recognize our capacities—that can be a discovery with some attraction for an individual who is getting tired of the hard slugging.

The role of the Weiss clique in the party is one of the purest examples of the destructiveness of such a clique operation in the leadership once it gets rolling, especially when part of its stock-in-trade is hiding behind a campaign to advance the interests of the oppressed.

How well have we done?

The objective weight of the ruling-class offensive on women's rights has been felt quite broadly. But we should note one other thing.

So far we have weathered the pressures of this period as well as any organization on the left, and far better than most. It's helpful to see the SWP in relation to the rest of the Fourth International especially, because there at least we have the common political framework of the resolution adopted at the 1979 World Congress.

Many of the larger sections and sympathizing organizations in the International have lost women from their membership and leadership to a greater degree than we have. We have a higher percentage of women in the party today, and more women who play central political leadership roles, than most other parties in the International. I don't say that with any sense of SWP-smugness. To the contrary, we would be very happy if it weren't true. We don't have "a crisis" on this question in the SWP. Some sections do.

There are three reasons why we have weathered these pressures relatively better than others:

1) The most important is the turn. Making the turn to the industrial working class and its organizations when we did established the political axis and framework of party building for our entire movement. It enabled us to avoid the crisis of perspective and directionless drift that has marked so many other radical organizations the last few years. Within this context, many women comrades played a particularly important role. We gained from being part of the organized union movement. And we were also part of the real vanguard of our class, and of women, when it came to fighting for affirmative action and the right of women to have access to jobs from which we were previously excluded. This gave us some real confidence born of rich experiences as part of our class.

2) The leadership school and education work within the party more generally. The boost of confidence that women comrades attending the school have gained from having the opportunity to seriously study Marx and Engels came at a crucial time for us. The Lenin classes in the party branches have played a similar role for many of us. Again there is a general lesson here that also applies to male comrades, but it has a bigger impact on women's self-confidence simply because we tend to start off with less. The fact that the party is today more communist, more politically homogeneous, affects us all.

In line with some of the earlier points we were discussing I think it is also useful to note how many comrades, women and men, with children and family responsibilities have attended the school. We took it for granted that we had a special responsibility to minimize the obstacles that comrades with kids faced in getting free for six months, and we organized accordingly. But especially for women with young children, it means even more to have such a chance to study.

3) The basic political grounding and education of our cadres in a materialist understanding of women's oppression. The standards in the party on this have always been high. No one is around the party for long without beginning to get educated on this question, without learning that it is an issue of first-rate importance to the working class.

This is one place, however, where we do have room for improvement today. It's not the purpose of this report to lay out an educational program. We need to think about it and propose a concrete program of study. But it is in order today to step up our educational work on women's oppression, including going back to Marx and Engels, and using more of the things that Evelyn wrote, which many comrades who have joined in the last six or seven years probably have not read.

Back to the election of the National Committee

The report has digressed a ways from its main focus, in order to come back to it with a better understanding of the challenges we're facing. I want to conclude by reiterating the three proposals made at the beginning of the report on the election of the National Committee.

1) That there be no change in the size of the National Committee at this convention.

2) That the convention use alternate membership on the National Committee, especially the bottom two-thirds of the list, to bring onto the NC a substantial number of comrades who are not currently members. This should include both younger party members who have demonstrated their potential to develop as future party leaders, and comrades who, regardless of age, are currently playing a leadership role in branches and fractions across the country. The purpose is to give such comrades, irrespective of previous membership on the committee, the opportunity to go through a year or two's experience as NC members allowing the party to further test them as well as benefit from their experience.

3) That we reaffirm and apply our general leadership criteria in the election of the National Committee. This means that we neither have quotas on the NC for comrades who are oppressed under capitalism for reasons of class, race, or sex; nor do we turn a blind-eye to the reality of this oppression or ignore our responsibility to take special measures to encourage such comrades to realize their full leadership potential.

We have not devoted so much of this report to a discussion of the question of women in the party because we expect—or think we need to accept—that there will be a decline in the numbers of women on the National Committee. There is no reason to anticipate that there will be fewer female candidates for membership on the National Committee. But the party also doesn't make any utopian demands on itself. We know that attrition takes its toll. Our approach must simply be one of continuing to apply and implement our affirmative action norms, while consciously working to maximize the opportunities for all comrades to stretch themselves as far as possible and take on the greatest leadership responsibilities they can.

As we prepare for the 1985 convention, the key is understanding what we achieved at the last convention, and what that now puts us in a better position to move forward to accomplish.

FORGING THE LEADERSHIP OF A PROLETARIAN PARTY
Excerpt from report adopted by SWP National Committee, May 1979

by Mary-Alice Waters

The election of the National Committee at the upcoming convention of the party will be one of the most important items of business before the delegates. The Political Committee thought it would be useful to have a separate report and discussion on the question of leadership development so we can prepare the party to move forward on this level as well.

A second, much briefer, part of this report is on the election of the Political Committee to serve between now and the convention. I will take that up at the end.

The starting point for our discussion of the development and selection of the party's leadership is the report, "Leading the Party Into Industry," adopted at the February 1978 plenum. The last part of that report deals with the leadership question.

I won't repeat what was outlined in that report on the leadership question. Comrades should re-read it. It provides the framework to advance our understanding of the job we face in constructing the leadership of the party.

Our starting point is the character of the coming American revolution and the strategic goals of our class that flow from it. The kind of leadership we must develop is determined by the kind of party it will take to lead that revolution. It will be a proletarian revolution to establish a workers government. Thus the party that leads that revolution must be a proletarian party. It cannot be a "combined party." It cannot be a coalition of sectors. There are not multiple vanguards. Our party must be the vanguard of the working class in program, composition, and collective experience. It must include in its ranks the most conscious vanguard fighters of the proletariat. Its composition must reflect the vanguard role of Black workers and the growing number of women workers, especially those who are fighting their way into sections of industry previously closed to women.

Once we have defined the character of the coming American revolution, and clarified the class character and composition of the party needed to lead that revolution, we must ask ourselves: What stage are we at right now in the construction of that party? What are the challenges and the tasks we face today? How do we go about transforming a cadre party of some 1,500 members—very few of whom are from working-class backgrounds, most of whom were recruited as students around the various social protest actions of the 1960s and early 1970s—into a party of industrial workers? Where are we in relation to our goal of transforming the membership and the leadership? Transforming the milieu in which we live and work? Transforming the axis of our work and making it revolve around our industrial fractions? Beginning to recruit young workers who will develop as leaders of our party?

What is leadership?

What is leadership in a Bolshevik party?

Our answer must start not with party leadership but with the party itself. In other words, we start with the leadership of the working class.

What is a *member* of a Bolshevik party? It's hard to come up with a better initial definition than the one Marx and Engels set forth in the *Communist Manifesto*. Communists "have no interests separate and apart from those of the working class as a whole."

That's what members of our party are. Individuals who subordinate everything to centralized collaboration with others who share and are totally committed to our revolutionary goals and perspectives. Individuals who strive in a disciplined way to help the party lead the working class to realize its historic tasks, which are the interests of all humanity.

In the party we're building, each and every member is a leader, a leader of the working class, part of the conscious vanguard of our class. We strive to maximize the political capacities and develop the leadership abilities of every single member. That's what we mean by a cadre party: a party in which all members are trained as leaders and are prepared to train others as leaders of their class. In other words, for us leadership is not an individual question, it is the question of the party itself.

This is a fundamental point. It's worth stopping to think about. It is the opposite of everything we are taught by class society. The party is made up of individuals, of course. But our strength is in our collectivity, not our individuality. Our strength is in our ability to function together as a team, as a machine. John G. Wright called it a thinking machine. It's a thinking machine, it's an acting machine, but it's a machine.

In this sense, too, we are like our class, because the strength of our class also lies in its collective power. Every worker knows that individually he or she has very little power. But together we can change the world. Solidarity, cooperation, and collaboration are the essence of strength.

This is the opposite of the consciousness created by bourgeois and petty-bourgeois conditions of life. For the bourgeoisie and petty bourgeoisie, success *does* depend on individual action. You come out on top only by pitting yourself against and defeating everybody else. Competition, not collective effort, is the precondition for survival. And for the bourgeoisie, the rewards all come from the exploitation of another class.

In the proletarian party, our concern about developing individuals as leaders is not to promote egocentric "self-fulfillment," but to increase our collective strength and advance the party and our class. That is what gives each of us as individuals a great deal of satisfaction.

This is why a Bolshevik party ultimately cannot be forged outside the conditions of life and the day-to-day living struggles of our class. This is why it must be proletarian in composition as well as in program.

Thus we arrive at the first criterion of leadership in a Bolshevik party: the ability to see ourselves in relationship to the party, not the party in relationship to ourselves. We derive our personal satisfaction from helping make the machine run, not from seeing our names up in neon lights. Our pride is in what the party does well, maximizing the results of that collective effort. Our reward is in advancing the party, not advancing ourselves as individuals competing for greater recognition from others.

We discussed this at our plenum a year ago in reference to the development of strong industrial fractions. Our aim, we said, is not to somehow try to ensure that every party member will become an outstanding individual leader of big working-class battles. That's an impossible goal, and an unnecessary one. Those natural leaders of the class are important, of course, and the SWP is training some of them today and will recruit more.

But that's not what's decisive for the party or for the class. That's not why we're so determined to get the overwhelming majority of party members and leaders into industry.

What is decisive, we've explained, is never what an individual comrade can accomplish on the job, whatever his or her strengths and weaknesses, but what the fraction accomplishes. More than that, it is what the national fraction accomplishes. And every single comrade in those fractions makes a contribution to that joint effort.

The effectiveness of the party depends on what we can do as a team through the branches, locals, fractions, committees, and leadership bodies. That is the kind of party our class needs to take it forward.

The National Committee

The fact that the party is a machine made up of cadres who function as a collective unit is one of the reasons why we stress that leadership of the party is much broader than the members of the National Committee.

The National Committee is the leading *committee* of the party. It is selected by the membership on the basis of both the general political capacities and the proven abilities of the individual members to lead the struggles through which the party is being built at any given stage. But it is put together as a committee, as a team. The core of the committee are the most tested and experienced leaders of the party over an extended period of time, but the team is and must constantly be renewed and changed. It is a living organism that grows and develops as the party and our class change and go through new experiences.

The National Committee is a team that incorporates comrades who are politically experienced in and lead diverse aspects of party activity—comrades carrying administrative responsibility, writers, speakers, organizers, mass workers, and so on. It includes different generations, different layers and experiences of the working class. In putting together the committee, we try to look ahead to where we're going, as well as to take account of where we've come from.

Above all, the National Committee is not a list of individuals. It is a *committee* in which the membership has political confidence as the leadership of the party.

In the course of the discussion here at this plenum, a number of comrades have referred to the new Education for Socialists bulletin entitled "Background to 'The Struggle for a Proletarian Party.'" This valuable bulletin contains, along with other items, a selection of letters Trotsky wrote to American comrades in 1937. Most of the letters dealt with the leadership question. We were starting to make a turn to the industrial working class then, and Trotsky was hammering away at us to speed it up. I'm sure those of you who have had a chance to read the bulletin have been struck by how timely and relevant it is.

In his letters, as later in *In Defense of Marxism,* Trotsky refers over and over again to the tendency toward "individualism" on the part of the petty-bourgeois members of the American party and of the old Russian Bolshevik Party. He points out that these are often very good comrades, but their attitudes are conditioned by their class experiences. He notes their tendency to criticize for the sake of criticism, to oppose for the sake of opposition, to doubt for the sake of covering their own deep skepticism concerning the revolutionary capacities of the working class. He contrasts these attitudes toward the party, and toward themselves, to the attitudes of working-class members.

Trotsky explained that seeing yourself in relation to the party—not the other way around—is a proletarian attitude.

To develop new leaders

Trotsky points to a second aspect of leadership in those letters as well.

Leaders are those who help others become leaders.

The party leadership has the responsibility to carefully prepare and thoroughly explain every decision, every policy, every shift, so that the membership is comfortable not only with what we are doing, but why. We try to work with and develop the self-confidence of every member as a thinking, experienced cadre who understands not just the tactics of the moment, but the fundamental strategic concepts that determine our always-changing tactics.

This concern to develop the capacities of every single member of the party and the leadership's political responsibilities toward the membership is summed up quite well when Trotsky said full-timers "of a revolutionary party should have in the first place a good ear, and only in the second place a good tongue."

Our need to help every single comrade develop her or his understanding and abilities is one of the reasons that we organize our work through committees and fractions. Of course, a committee or fraction functions better than an individual, since we all have our weaknesses. Working collectively, we try to balance each other and compensate for our weaknesses. That's obvious.

But working through fractions and committees is also how to develop comrades. We never put comrades all alone in an assignment and then say, "Well, that was over their head. They just couldn't handle it." Every assignment is a collective responsibility. Ultimately, the decisive test of how well we lead is how well we prepare our replacement, how well we pass on what we know and train somebody else to take over from us.

Affirmative action

Third, Trotsky explains that both proletarianizing the party and what we would today call affirmative action are indispensable to developing a proletarian leadership. He argues that conscious measures must be taken to increase the proletarian composition of the leading bodies of the party and to advance the self-confidence of young worker cadres as leaders. The key points he makes are along the lines that we've been discussing over the last few years in relationship to the development of leaders of the party who are Black and Latino and female.

Trotsky explains that if you just let nature take its course, given the composition and arenas of activity of many members, workers who aren't glib, with "general formulas and fluent pens,"—just rich in their "acquaintance with the life of workers and practical capacities"—are likely to be overlooked as part of the leadership. He proposed that a whole layer of such working-class cadres with proven abilities and capacities should be consciously placed on the National Committee and other leading bodies to strengthen the leadership politically and, at the same time, allow these comrades to develop. He points out that participation in the leading committees of the party is important in and of itself at a certain stage of a leader's education. Trotsky urged the party to cut through all the "secondary, factional, and personal conditions [that] play too great a role in the composition of the list of candidates" for the leading bodies of the party, and consciously renew the leadership through these kinds of affirmative-action measures.

Leadership and party democracy

Fourth, Trotsky explains that these concepts of leadership are inextricably interconnected with the question of party democracy.

He asks, What is party democracy? And he lists three elements.

1. "The strictest observance of the party statutes by the leading bodies"—regular conventions, full discussion periods, right of minorities to express their opinions, right to form tendencies, and so forth. All the things that are codified in our constitution and organizational principles. But, Trotsky writes, that is only the very beginning.

2. "A patient, friendly, to a certain point pedagogical attitude on the part of the central committee and its members toward the rank and file, including the objectors and the discontented, because it is not a great merit to be satisfied 'with anybody who is satisfied with me.'"

He goes on: "Methods of psychological 'terrorism,' including a haughty or sarcastic manner of answering or treating every objection, criticism, or doubt—it is, namely, this journalistic or 'intellectualistic' manner which is insufferable to workers and condemns them to silence." Eradicating this kind of conduct by "leaders" is also at the heart of party democracy.

But, Trotsky insists, these two elements still aren't enough. It is not sufficient merely to abide by formal rules of party democracy and outlaw terroristic methods or ridicule of comrades who raise questions and new ideas.

3. The leadership must also maintain "permanent, active, and informal contact with the rank and file, especially when a new slogan or a new campaign is in preparation or when it is necessary to verify the results of an accomplished campaign." The leading bodies, Trotsky says, must be "closely connected with the rank and file, organically representative of them."

Trotsky insisted that only that kind of party, with those kinds of conscious leadership attitudes, could make the turn to industrial workers that was necessary in 1937. And this holds for us in 1979.

Finally, we should add what we have stressed before. Leaders are those who willingly shoulder broad general political responsibility—beyond whatever specific assignments they have, regardless of what "posts," if any, they have. To put it most simply, leadership is not what assignment you take but how you carry out whatever's necessary. Leaders are those who lead.

These are some of the basic concepts about the party and about party leadership that the SWP had learned from Trotsky and from our own experiences by the end of the 1930s. The basic cadre of our party absorbed these attitudes and was able to pass them on without a break in continuity. That has been decisive in enabling us to go as far as we have in assembling—in a qualitatively different way than most of the other parties of the Fourth International—a homogeneous leadership team, composed of comrades of different generations, men and women, and comrades of oppressed nationalities. The success we have had in this is based on these most fundamental proletarian attitudes toward the party and leadership. It has allowed us, among other things, to carry through an unprecedented transition in leadership.

Some proletarian attitudes

Many of these lessons—and a few others, too—were touched on by Farrell Dobbs in his tribute to Joe Hansen. We published Farrell's remarks to the San Francisco memorial meeting a few weeks ago in *Intercontinental Press*. [April 16, 1979]

Farrell pointed to Joe's understanding that leadership is not what you do but how you do it. He capsulized this in the story of how Joe took the assignment of *Militant* business manager after the Cochranites bellyached about having a leader of their faction asked to take such a politically unimportant "technical" assignment. Joe carried out that assignment in a serious and professional way. He loved it. And he loved demonstrating to the whole party that every single assignment is important.

Farrell was paying Joe one of his highest tributes when he called him a "disciplined soldier." Someone who knew that everything we do—whether organizing a branch, serving as the SWP observer on the United Secretariat, promoting the circulation of our press, getting a job in steel—is all just working as part of the team. We are all thinking, acting, disciplined pieces in a much bigger thinking and acting machine. As Joe used to say, "It's all labor power." Everything we do is part of building the party. That's what counts.

Secondly, Farrell emphasized Joe's self-control and self-discipline. Especially under pressure, sometimes enormous pressure, whether in Mexico in Trotsky's household, or working to hold the party together throughout the period of McCarthyism in this country. Joe never "lost his cool," Farrell said.

Third, Joe was supremely conscious that leaders have a general responsibility for maintaining the equilibrium of the party. They take the party seriously. If you have an idea or a proposal or something that you think is wrong, you don't just pop off with it, no matter what the time of day. As Farrell put it, you don't "start making a racket like a mule in a tin barn" when you have a difference.

You raise your ideas, criticism, proposals, in a balanced way, at the correct time and place, and with a sense of proportion about the needs of the entire party. The more leadership responsibility you carry, the more your actions and opinions can have an impact on the stability and the equilibrium of the party and its ability to function.

In one of the letters I mentioned earlier, Trotsky recalled Lenin's view on this matter. When Lenin called for Ordzhonikidze to be expelled from the party in 1923, Trotsky wrote, "he said very correctly that the discontented party member has the right to be turbulent, but not a member of the central committee." Farrell noted that Joe always acted like a leader in this respect and understood that leaders have less right, not greater leeway, to indulge their "individualism," their personal whims and foibles.

Fourth, Farrell stressed that Joe wasn't one of those people who try to show how brilliant they are by trying to make others seem stupid. Joe didn't try to prove he was an "independent thinker" by refusing to learn from Trotsky. The result was that he was able to learn. He learned how to think through whatever problem was before him, to approach questions systematically, to see all the different angles, and to solve those problems.

The leadership qualities Farrell pointed to in Joe are not inherent qualities in anyone. They are things that everyone can learn. They are acquired proletarian attributes of leadership that we all can develop.

Leaders who are Black, Latino, and female

I want to turn now to a specific aspect of the leadership question that we have been discussing since the last convention: the challenge we face in developing Black and Latino and women comrades as rounded leaders of the party.

We should add that in the 1980's, we will face a similar challenge in developing young workers we recruit out of the plants. Many of them will be Black, Latino, and women as well.

The special challenges we face in developing this kind of leadership are real. But 99% of the answers are to be found in the general approach we have to all leadership questions.

We should begin by separating the questions of developing leaders from the oppressed nationalities and developing leaders who are women. Some aspects are similar, but there are differences as well.

Let's start with the challenge facing us in the development of Blacks, Chicanos, Puerto Ricans, and other comrades of oppressed national minorities. Beginning with the report and discussion at the February 1978 plenum, we have come to a much clearer understanding of why a party that is genuinely multinational in its ranks and its leadership cannot be built unless it is proletarian in composition and milieu. A proletarian program alone is not sufficient.

We can, of course, assemble a vanguard around our program, as we have done in the last decade and a half. The scope of this recruitment and development of Black and Latino comrades is an accomplishment new in the history of American Trotskyism. As we turn to the new political openings in the industrial working class, this accomplishment will enable us to better recruit and integrate young Black and Latino workers.

But the next step forward in the construction of a multinational leadership can only be taken by a party whose members are part of the industrial working class. Why do we say this?

So long as the party was composed primarily of students and white-collar, semiprofessional workers, and the radicalization took the form of social protest actions in which the mass organizations of the working class played little role, it was more difficult to overcome the deep suspicions of Blacks and Latinos attracted to us. It was more difficult to recruit comrades of oppressed nationalities than to recruit whites. This was true because in addition to all the other obstacles—which still make the recruitment of every individual exceptional—the class milieu in which we functioned, the petty-bourgeois conditions of life, maximized conflicts of interests.

There is no way around the fact that for white students—especially those from petty-bourgeois backgrounds, but from working-class families as well—there are invariably choices and options not open to Blacks and Latinos. This is true for comrades as well.

Most white comrades have had the experience of working to recruit a Black or Latino contact and being asked—sometimes openly, sometimes implicitly—"You *say* you stand on this program, but how do I know you mean it? Will you really be around when the going gets tough? What's in it for you?"

The issues around which the radicalization was deepening, and the conditions of struggle, didn't always provide a lot of opportunities to prove that we weren't just idealistic supporters of good causes. So we recruited only those Blacks and Latinos who were able to overcome tremendous objective barriers. They had to be exceptionally clear-sighted and tough.

Those kinds of obstacles are diminished, though, as the party becomes proletarian not only in program but in composition and milieu. The relations between Black and white workers on the picket line in Newport News are different from the relations between Black and white radicals on the campus. The relationship between Black and white comrades on the line in an auto plant are different than in an antiwar coalition.

Solidarity is the precondition of survival in the working class. Your common class interests are obviously great, despite the national oppression that one worker suffers and another doesn't. You have the same material interests as members of the same class. And that is what comes to the fore, especially in periods of struggle.

Moreover, as the class polarization deepens, it becomes clearer that the road forward for both the Black liberation struggle and the labor movement are inseparably intertwined. Both the forces necessary to win Black rights, and the Black leadership whose class understanding and political courage will make possible the next stage of struggle, will be found in the mills, the factories, the ship yards, etc. You don't have to choose between fighting for the needs of Black people or transforming the labor movement. The forging of a class-struggle left wing in the unions and the revitalization of an uncompromising movement for Black rights are intertwined.

Attitudes begin to change in struggle. Mutual confidence is forged among the best fighters, among those who lead. You're not supporting a good program. You're fighting to your own common needs. The answer to "What's in this for you or me?" is obvious. It becomes not a choice, but a necessity.

It's only under these conditions that a broad

multinational composition and leadership—not just a thin layer, but a broad-based cadre—can be built. The leaders and members of the SWP must have unshakeable confidence in each other. We have to be prepared to put our lives in each others' hands. And that kind of party can only be forged in real proletarian class combat. It becomes obvious why the party must be politically homogeneous and steeled through common leadership experience in the class struggle.

We should also keep in mind an important objective change that makes our perspective of building this kind of party realistic. The kind of *multinational* party and leadership that must be built today could not have been built several decades ago because the composition of the proletariat itself was not the same. During World War II, and in the postwar years, massive urbanization and proletarianization of the oppressed nationalities took place.

In the 1930s the Black population and the Chicano population were much more rural and engaged in agriculture. They were more an ally of the working class than a layer of the working class. This has changed dramatically over the past forty years.

Of course, you had to have a multinational party in the 1930s, too. You had to have the correct line on Black self-determination. You had to have a correct understanding of the vanguard role that the Black proletariat would play. And we did.

But the degree and the extent to which the forging of a broad multinational cadre is both possible and a life-or-death question to the American revolution is different today than it was fifty years ago. And it becomes more crucial each passing year, as the proletarianization of the oppressed nationalities continues.

That is why it is both more necessary and more possible today to construct a proletarian party that is multinational in composition and leadership. It's important to keep this in mind as we look back and evaluate the history of our own party.

But the fact that it is more possible to build a multinational party today, as well as more vital to the future of humanity, does not mean it will happen automatically.

It doesn't eliminate the extra barriers created by this society—barriers that must be overcome in the development of leaders of the party who are Black, or who are Chicano, or Puerto Rican, or any oppressed national minority. It doesn't mean that we no longer have to take special measures to encourage the development of Black and Latino comrades as party leaders.

That's why we have and will continue to have a policy of affirmative action, that is, of consciously encouraging and giving special attention to the leadership development of comrades of the oppressed nationalities.

But these special steps now take place within the framework of our turn into industry, of our progress towards building a more proletarian party. As Blacks and Latinos gain confidence as leaders of the working class, they will also become more self-confident as leaders of the vanguard party of our class.

Blacks and Latinos will be in the forefront of those workers who push toward a class-struggle left wing in the unions. They will fight to unify the class around a program that champions the demands of all the oppressed and exploited. They will provide the proletarian leadership necessary to revitalize massive social protests for Black and Latino rights.

Through these experiences, and as part of a revolutionary combat party, they will participate in leading the mass proletarian actions that will culminate in the conquest of power and the establishment of a workers government.

This is the perspective that the SWP can and does offer the Black and Latino workers we are talking to and working with as we get into industry. This is the road to the development of a multinational proletarian party.

Party leaders who are women

What about developing leaders of the party who are women?

Most of what we've said so far applies to women. But we also have to say more.

We face the challenge of building a party and leadership unlike anything that has ever existed before. That's a historical fact. And the explanation is simple. The sex composition of the American working class today is unlike anything that has existed before. The changes on this level are similar to what we were just saying about the race question.

A party with the sex composition of the Bolshevik Party of 1917 could not lead the American revolution today. There was not a single woman in the central political leadership of the Bolshevik Party. Krupskaya may have been one of the strongest women, but she was never a member of the central committee. Kollantai played an important role, but she was not a rounded political leader, never carried any general central leadership responsibility.

I think that if you look back cold-bloodedly on the history of the Marxist movement, you would have to say that there is really only one woman who stands out as that kind of central political leader—Rosa Luxemburg. Perhaps it would be correct to include Eleanor Marx, too.

But if Luxemburg was unique in the history of the Marxist movement, that is not something we need to be defensive or apologetic about. It is no fault of Marxism or Leninism or the leaderships of genuine Marxist and Leninist parties.

Rather, it is a result of two historical factors: first, the stage of development of capitalism itself and the sex composition of the workforce; and second, the depth of women's oppression, institutionalized through the family, and the profound affect this has on the character structure of every female raised in class society.

If we who live in the economically strongest capitalist countries, in the last part of the twentieth century, can be relatively optimistic about our ability to build a party and leadership that is different in leadership composition from anything that has existed so far, it is because of the changes produced by the development of capitalism itself.

The post–World War II economic expansion, with its great acceleration in the 1960s, brought about a qualitative increase in the percentage of women in the labor market: in the United States it is now more than 60% of women between the ages of 18 and 55. It brought about a qualitative increase in the percentage of the labor force who are women: it is now more than 40%. These changes, more than any other *single* factor, underlie the "second wave" of feminist struggle.

Moreover—and most important for us—women have begun over the past decade to bust down the barriers to entering the sectors of industry from which they were previously excluded. This is new. It has happened since the late 1960s. And when the next bad recession hits, the working class will have a real battle to prevent these women from being driven out of industry.

These changes are decisive for the development of women who are leaders of the working class, and the creation of a proletarian party of the kind our tasks require. And our turn gives us a new framework to advance the political self-confidence of women comrades. Many comrades who have gotten industrial jobs in the last months have already experienced this.

When you go from working as a personal secretary and servant for some man in an office, to an auto assembly line, the change affects your own consciousness. It affects your attitudes towards yourself and what you're capable of doing.

Getting out of the isolation and dependency of the home and into the work force is a gigantic step for women that changes consciousness. But taking the next step into sectors of industry previously closed to women is now even more crucial to the development of the kind of leadership we need.

As women bust down the barriers to industry, you also see changes—often rapid changes—in the attitudes of men on the assembly lines or in the steel plants. They see the women they are working with in a different light. Sexist prejudices begin to break down.

A party with a significant component of women in its central leadership cannot be built except as a working class party—in composition as well as program. We can say this definitively. It is not a question of individuals. We're not saying that only women who are workers can overcome the barriers and develop as leaders. But a revolutionary *party* with a broad cadre of leaders who are women can only be forged in the real battles of our class, and this will be totally intertwined with the changing composition of the industrial labor force.

Women have a deep fear of leadership. We are conditioned from the day we're born to fear the consequences of attempting to lead—to lead men, especially. We are taught that such a course will inevitably mean loneliness and personal rejection by men. That no man can tolerate a challenge to his "masculinity" by an independent, self-confident woman who acts as a leader. And few men can.

This is the biggest obstacle to the development

of women leaders. It is rooted in the character structure, the psychology, of the oppressed sex. It is something that every woman faces and has to deal with.

This is why the development of women as leaders is even more of a challenge than developing Black and Latino leaders of the party. Of course, for Latinas and Black women, these factors are compounded. The challenge for them is even greater.

The changes in women's consciousness and self-confidence will go hand in hand with changing attitudes among men. Men will lose their fear of being challenged by women as women gain the economic independence and psychological self-confidence to become leaders of men. And that's one of the reasons why the changes in our class, the affirmative-action battles we are winning, are so important. It is a question of the future of humanity—male and female.

The SWP leadership today

How is all this reflected in the leadership of the party today? The progress we have made as well as the obstacles we have yet to overcome, are indicated by the composition of the National Committee elected at the last convention. The membership of the SWP is roughly 42% female, but 33% of the National Committee is women. On the other hand, 6 or 7% of party members are Black but 26% of our National Committee is Black. The Latino members make up about 5% of the party, and about 7% of the National Committee.

As of this plenum, about 39% of the membership, and 30% of the National Committee are industrial workers.

My own opinion is that the composition of our National Committee is not out of harmony with the real leadership of the party. Give or take a few percentage points—and that is not important—those figures fairly accurately register what we have accomplished. In that sense, the National Committee elected at the last convention is good. Because, as we pointed out at the time, our elected leadership and our real leadership had better coincide, or else our leading committees would lose their authority. We would be as phony as a three-dollar bill if our real leadership and our elected leadership got out of mesh.

But I want to talk about something else. What is behind those statistics? What do they tell us about the party? We should take a look at this in relation to the need for the party to take special steps to aid and to challenge women comrades to develop leadership capacities.

This is one of the questions that came up during the discussion on the election of the NC at our August 1977 convention.

But it was posed in the wrong framework. Election to the NC was seen as a solution to leadership questions, rather than as a register of where we are. We all sensed there was something wrong with that discussion. We were uncomfortable with it. But why did it happen?

In part, we in the leadership fostered it. At the convention we called attention to the fact that there was a significant discrepancy between the percentage of the party that is female and the percentage of women on the National Committee. And we indicated that we thought that the new NC would register the continuing progress we had made in the development of leaders who are women. But we didn't say anything more. We didn't discuss, "Why is there a discrepancy of this kind? Where does it come from? Does it mean women aren't getting adequate consideration in nominations for the NC? What step do we need to take?"

As a result, there was a tendency to give the easy answers, to look for the easy solutions. That's natural. But when the problems are hard, easy answers don't get you very far. And they often point in the wrong direction.

One easy answer is to approach the leadership as a sum total of categories and percentages, rather than thinking about the real leadership of the party. That is, to start with trying to make the statistics look the way we'd like them to, not with the election of a committee to politically lead the party. Many comrades hoped the nominating commission would rectify the *percentages.* When there was still a discrepancy (though a smaller one), comrades were disappointed. They felt that a mistake had been made. That was how we got into the situation where, by a closely divided vote, the delegates decided on the spot to enlarge the NC by five. Of course, that's in order and not necessarily a mistake. There are always many comrades qualified to serve on the NC beyond those put forward by the nominating commission to open the nominations.

But the discussion took place within a false framework that assumed the election of the NC is itself a way of developing leadership. It isn't. It can't be. All it can do is *register*, as accurately and objectively as the human beings who are the convention delegates are capable of doing, the progress we have made *before* we get to the convention. Of course, the convention can push things a little bit in the right direction—but only a little bit. If it tries to push too far, it can come up with a list of nominations that does not accurately reflect the real leadership of the party.

The task of developing leadership is not the job of the nominating commission, or the delegates to the convention. It is a job that begins on the branch level, in every single party committee and fraction.

Misconceptions about what can be accomplished in the election of the NC are closely related to another easy answer. Does the fact that women are a smaller percentage of the National Committee than of the membership indicate that women are not being given due consideration for the NC? Put more broadly, does the *party* place obstacles or barriers in the way of the development of women as leaders? Does the *party* restrict women comrades to certain kinds of assignments, certain roles? If that were true, then the solution would be simple. Just remove the barriers in the party.

But this is false. The record of the nominating commissions at the last conventions unambiguously indicates that women are given *preferential* consideration for election to the NC. And I think that is generally true at all levels, and for most assignments in the party. I would say, moreover, that in relationship to other organizations of our class, our leadership is excellent on this score. And everyone knows it is *real*.

If, even with preferential consideration given to leaders who are women, the percentage of women on the NC is lower than the percentage of women in the party, this tells us we have a bigger challenge to overcome, a bigger problem to face up to in developing women as rounded political leaders. There is no reason for us to be defensive about this. We are dealing with the way *society* perpetuates the oppression of women. What women are taught and conditioned to believe about themselves from the day they are born. Women don't overcome that just by joining the SWP, or understanding our program.

There are many women who are leaders in our party. We all know that. Moreover, there has been a marked expansion of the leadership responsibilities of women in recent years. The women's liberation movement had a deep impact on all of us, female and male. For example, the number of women who are organizers and candidates, write for our press, and carry out other important assignments is qualitatively greater today than twenty years ago.

But we also know something else. There is a tendency for women to develop as leaders of a certain kind, as organizers who do a good job of organizing the campaigns of the party, working with comrades, pulling things together. But often women tend to reach a plateau at some stage that they can't go beyond because they're not politically equipped. It is not enough to understand tactics, or to be able to explain our position on this or that, or to be good at working with people.

All party leaders—men and women—have to become thorough Marxists. Have to be politically grounded with an understanding of our broad strategic perspectives and learn how to apply them to the diverse situations and challenges we face today. Have to develop that kind of political self-confidence and learn to think politically in clear class terms.

If there is a tendency for women comrades to develop as leaders of a certain type, it is not because the party fosters it. The problem lies much deeper. All the social pressure and the psychological conditioning of women push us in that direction. The institutions of class society work to produce in us a deeply ingrained lack of self-confidence. After all, society doesn't take us seriously; why should we consider ourselves important?

So we often shy away from the broadest, general leadership responsibilities. Consciously or not we often hide in a narrower, more comfortable niche, where we feel less pressure. We become very good, become real leaders, in some aspect of party functioning. And we derive satisfaction from knowing we are doing something well, that it's important, that we are leading.

But, at the same time, we can't fool ourselves. We know what we're doing.

Feminist laments

We all know the signs of this that bother us. We feel uncomfortable when few delegates who are women take the floor at conventions whenever the discussion is on broad general, political questions. We often go to each other and say, "Hey, why don't you speak on this?"

We're dissatisfied with the number of women who write for our press. But it's the same challenge as the convention debates. Women comrades more often than men lack the general political self-confidence that comes from the combination of experience and systematically making time to read, to absorb in the light of new events things we may or may not have read before by Marx, and Engels, and Lenin and Trotsky. In order to write clearly, you have to understand clearly, to be able to explain what you understand to others.

And we're unhappy that despite preferential consideration, there are not significantly more women on the National Committee.

But sometimes we hide the central problem, our own tendency to pull back from shouldering general political leadership responsibility, by what I call feminist laments. Why isn't a woman doing this or that? Why aren't we being recognized?

In the Fourth International you sometimes hear it in extreme forms. Some comrades express the idea that Leninism itself is a "male" concept of leadership that inherently oppresses women; that women are by nature leaders of a different kind than men.

We can't allow our feminist consciousness to become an excuse to hide behind, rather than an aid to us in thinking out how to meet the challenge we face. In order to survive in capitalist society, women have learned to act in certain ways. That is, you know you never get a fair shake; that whatever abilities you may have will never be the reason you do or don't "get ahead"; that you have to shoot every angle, fake it, sell yourself; and that if you do it right, you can go a long way. If we act like that toward the party, it can only lead to a self-defeating disaster and a self-perpetuating "women problem."

Each and every one of us was born and raised in capitalist society, and we have all the problems and hang-ups that come with that. But the party *is* different from capitalist society in general. Our conscious goal, as we discussed earlier, is to work together collectively to maximize the political development of every comrade. The real pressure on women in the SWP is not that we are held back but that we are constantly pressed to take on greater and greater responsibility.

At the same time, no one in the party can fake it politically, not in the long run. Either we become self-confident and rounded Marxists, or we reach a limit before too long. The party is too serious, and women and men in the SWP are too serious, to tolerate anything that is phony.

A personal challenge

The most important question is: "What are we going to do to move forward on this front?"

The first thing is to frankly discuss the real challenge before us and not try to hide behind false explanations and fake solutions. It should give us a great deal of confidence that we *can* squarely confront this and apply the same materialist analysis and class perspective that we apply to every other question before our party and our class. There are no phony solutions. There are no organizational cure-alls.

We are not going to change the character structure of the oppressed sex—or of men either—between now and the revolution. But that is no excuse for not moving decisively to affect the conditions we can. Just the opposite. Being clear about the nature of the obstacles we face is the first step.

Second, there is a personal challenge before every single woman in the party. Whatever the party does collectively to help educate and maximize the political development of every individual, at a certain point there is one and only one thing that makes a difference: our own individual determination to educate ourselves. We all have to begin by recognizing that we have to combine our day-to-day activities and experiences in the class struggle with reading, studying, learning to think every political question through for ourselves. No one else can do it for us.

Education in our movement doesn't come from ivory tower study. We don't decide: Okay, I'm going to learn how to think like a Marxist, so I'll go off somewhere by myself and read the classics for a year or two. We can educate ourselves only in the course of the living experiences we go through in the class struggle, and how we respond to them.

When the revolution in Iran comes along, or the events in Southeast Asia, or the Newport News strike, we get excited. We try to think through, "What does this mean about the class struggle nationally, internationally? What does this change? What are the class forces at work? How should revolutionists respond?" The answers are not always obvious. So we go to our bookshelf and pick up a few books, to read or reread, to think about what is happening. If we don't do that, if we aren't politically inspired by what is happening and what we're doing, if we don't *want* to read and study—then no one else can do it for us. No one else can pick up that book. No one else can force us to *make* time. No one else can read it for us, think about it for us, study it for us.

Is this a *personal* challenge? Yes.

Is it harder for women to do this? Yes, it's harder. That is a historical fact, a fact of life in class society.

Are many problems that we used to think were personal shortcomings, really not our own fault? Yes.

But then, we have to add, *so what?*

Because it is harder for us, do we think it is less necessary? Do we think the standards of leadership for us should be lower than for men? Do we think there can be some definition of leadership for women that is different than for men? Of course not. We know that nothing would be more patronizing, degrading, or insulting to women in the party.

At a certain point, each one of us has to face up to the challenge, and decide to work to overcome it. It is that simple. We can all be very supportive and understanding of each other's problems and difficulties. We can recognize they are largely created by the society in which we live. But that is not going to help lead the American revolution—unless we also challenge each other to overcome the obstacles, to face up to the real needs of our sex and our class, and to see our responsibilities in that light.

A collective challenge

Of course this doesn't mean women must meet this challenge only as individuals. The party as a whole has responsibilities, too. We think that one of the most important things we can and must do in the near future is establish the full-time cadre school, the leadership school that we have talked about before—Sandstone University, or whatever we decide to call it. We need to systematically take leaders of the party, in small groups, relieve them of other responsibilities, and give them several months for organized, intensive study.

There are always many reasons why we "can't" do this right now: we don't have the money, we're too tight on personnel, there are too many other responsibilities, and so on. But the Political Committee is proposing that we now cut through all those problems—which, of course, are real—and decide that we can't afford *not* to do this. Now.

We thought that the Evelyn Reed Scholarship Fund was a good way to start collecting the money necessary to finance this project. We will have to raise a significant amount to carry it through, and we have to find the resources outside our normal operating budget. If comrades agree, we will make this the center of the expansion fund presentation at the convention, and we will plan to hold the opening session of this school before our 1980 Oberlin conference. If we are serious about this, we think we will find the extra money needed to do it.

Second, the party as a whole has the responsibility to continue a policy of affirmative action to encourage women and comrades of the oppressed nationalities to overcome the additional obstacles they face. As with every member, our aim is to stretch comrades' capacities to the fullest, to encourage them to take assignments that challenge them to grow, and then to work collectively to maximize what we accomplish and learn in the process.

Third, we need to continue to do everything we can to maximize the number of women comrades who are in industry. Women in the party must help lead the turn into industry, where we can gain experience as leaders of our class. After getting off to a slow start, we've done well on this in recent months. Last summer, for example, there was only one woman on the National Committee in industry. There are now nine, and one more looking for a job. And I should add that four of these nine comrades are Black women.

We should be absolutely clear that this general approach is the exact opposite of the course toward the establishment of women's caucuses in the party, and toward the "development" of leaders by setting aside quotas on the leading bodies for women, etc. The challenge before us—especially for the women—is not to organize and lead the women in the party, but to lead the whole party, the branches, the fractions, the committees, the men *and* the women. Any other kind of leadership is counterfeit. Exclusive caucuses, based on sex, race, or any similar nonpolitical criteria, are both undemocratic and counterproductive. Far from encouraging women to become leaders of the party, they reinforce the idea that there is a separate kind of leadership role for women comrades.

Preparing the convention

Now, what does all this say about preparations for the election of the National Committee at the next convention?

First, we think we should recommend to the Nominating Commission and to the convention delegates that there be no further increase in the size of the National Committee. We now have a National Committee of eighty-three members. It is the largest National Committee the party has ever had, and one of the youngest.

At the 1975 convention we made a major transition in leadership. We eliminated the category of advisory members on the National Committee. Since none of those who had been advisory members ran for the committee, and since we increased the number of full and alternate members, we in effect enlarged the National Committee by ten in 1975.

Then, we enlarged the National Committee by sixteen at the last convention: eleven regular members and five alternates. There was a particular reason for recommending that increase in the size of the NC at the 1977 convention that doesn't apply this year.

We had held three successive yearly conventions of the party in 1975, '76, and '77. We pointed out that a time period of only one year is often not sufficient for the party to judge the performance of new members of the NC. It's an error to replace people on the National Committee prematurely, without their having a chance to go through a number of experiences, and without the party really being able to gauge their leadership functioning. But it has been two years since the last convention, so this is less of a factor this year.

Enlarging the National Committee further will not help resolve the leadership question that we're trying to deal with.

Secondly, the delegates and the Nominating Commission will have before them the thinking on the leadership question contained in this report, and the report on the turn from the February 1978 plenum.

These establish a political framework for the Nominating Commission and the branch delegations in considering their NC nominations before the convention.

Most important, we should remember that the National Committee is a *committee*. Like the party, it is a living, changing, growing, and developing organism. It is constantly adjusting and being renewed. One thing you can be sure of is that no National Committee will be perfect. Every delegate will have some idea of how it could have been a better committee. But we should all have a sense of proportion and perspective. Over time, any mistakes that are made get corrected. The goal is to make sure that we elect a *committee* in which the party has political confidence.

I think we can be confident, more confident than ever before, in our ability to rise to the challenges before us. We have made progress that we can now build on. We have a clear and balanced approach to the leadership question, to leadership functioning, to revolutionary centralism and proletarianization, to aiding and accelerating the development of every single comrade as a leader. We start with the things we learned from Trotsky and Lenin, the things that have become part of the consciousness and practice of our party.

This gives us a tremendous advantage in moving forward the process of forging a multinational leadership. A leadership with a significant component of women. A leadership that reflects a party whose great majority are becoming industrial workers. A leadership with continuity, stability, and political authority. A leadership that is constantly growing and adjusting. We can be proud of what we've done, and confident we can do more. I am not talking about patting ourselves on the back, but taking advantage of what we have accomplished to lead the whole party forward in meeting the leadership challenge.

SUMMARY

A number of comrades discussed the question: What does it mean to develop rounded political leaders of the party? This is posed not only for women or for comrades from oppressed nationalities. It's *the* supreme challenge for every single member of the party, for every single leadership body, in everything we do. That's our reason for being, to develop every individual we recruit as a rounded Marxist politician and part of the leadership of our class.

We are *all* being pushed, collectively and individually, by the objective situation today, pushed to deepen our political understanding, to think through the questions being posed in a new way by the development of the class struggle.

The leadership is challenged to make every branch meeting a political meeting. To make every fraction meeting a political meeting.

We know there are additional obstacles and difficulties for women comrades and comrades from oppressed nationalities. This will be true for many comrades we recruit on the job in industry. We have to give special leadership attention to helping overcome these barriers, reinforcing comrades' self-confidence, and deepening their political understanding.

Caroline began to discuss the question, "What do we mean when we say 'political'?" That branch meetings have to be "political." Or comrades have to be more "political." This is important. Of course, no one joins the Socialist Workers Party unless they are a political being. There is no other reason to join a revolutionary Marxist party in the United States today.

Being political doesn't mean becoming a "theoretician." It doesn't mean trying to be an "intellectual" or an "educator." These are all false definitions.

What we're trying to get at is the fact that everything we do, every task we have—from the sale of our press, to the branch finances, to antinuclear work, to attending a trade-union meeting, to organizing the print shop of the party—every single thing we do has to be related to the broadest strategic goals of our class. That's the only reason we do anything. Only when we understand how our tasks today, what we are doing right now, this hour, are related to our ultimate goals, will we feel confident about where we're going, why it's all important. We always have to be forcing ourselves to think in broad class terms—because it's easy sometimes to sink into routinism, to give organizational, not political motivations for our tasks today. That's the heart of what we're trying to get at when we say our branch meetings and fraction meetings have to be "political."

We try to find ways to explain not *that* we need to sell the paper this week, but *why*. Ways to politically inspire comrades. Not inspire in the false sense—rah, rah, get everybody hepped up. That never works anyway, because there is really only one thing that motivates any of us. We get inspired by understanding where our class is going and how we are all going to help get there.

As Dick explained, Marxist theoreticians don't come from universities. Theory doesn't develop in a vacuum. It grows out of the class struggle itself, as the working class confronts new problems, as a proletarian party responds to the living class struggle.

That's why we don't urge comrades to go lock themselves up in a room alone to read the classics. You will *never* become a Marxist if you do that. Perhaps you will become very "well educated" in the bourgeois sense, but you will understand nothing about Marxism. You can only learn that by combining your reading and thinking with being a part of our class and its struggles, with being a member of a Marxist party. Some comrades aren't "organizers" while others are "educators." "Activists" aren't counterposed to "theoreticians." As Karen said, you can't be an organizer unless you understand and lead a branch or a fraction politically.

What is happening now is that we're being challenged to organize in a new way, to think through everything we do in relation to a new situation. That's what we mean when we say we have to be more political today. It's exciting to relate everything we're doing in a new way to the broadest strategic questions. We're all learning.

Another term we sometimes misuse is the word "intellectual." It comes from a time in the history of the Marxist movement when the majority of the working class couldn't read or write. Those who were educated, who could read or write, often played a very valuable role. It was important to win a section of the educated middle classes, the "intelligentsia," to the side of the working class and the workers movement.

But this distinction between intellectuals and non-intellectuals more and more disappears as the level of education in the working class rises. Someone who went to college, or can write an article on philosophy, or knows several languages is no longer an intellectual. Individuals make particular contributions to our collective efforts to develop our theoretical understanding or political position on one or another question. But the whole party is a thinking machine. It's out of the collective process that theory and our political positions develop.

Women in industry

Several comrades discussed the impact that working an industrial job has on the consciousness and self-confidence of women, including our own comrades.

Of course, all the comrades who get into industry find that we have to go back to the basics to rethink things. We have to explain our ideas to people in a new way. We have to deepen our understanding in order to be able to explain our positions in a popular way, to be understandable to the people we're meeting and talking to on the job today.

But getting into industry has an even greater impact on women comrades. Not only those who are already in, but on the whole party. Our self-confidence as leaders, the realization that we have power as part of our class, the sense of solidarity, the clarity about how we can build a powerful, fighting women's liberation movement that brings the power of the unions behind it—our consciousness is being transformed on many levels.

Marcia's point was accurate. Women in our party are used to being leaders. They already think and act like leaders. When our women comrades go into industry, they're not so likely to be cowed by things that might be more intimidating to other women. That growing self-confidence feeds back into the party as well.

There is a general point about our leadership needs that we have to begin to assess. We have been pressing hard to get the maximum number of comrades into industry. This has put a tremendous leadership strain on us. We have bent the stick toward getting as many leaders in as possible. But we're starting to reach the point where we will have to take comrades out—to meet some leadership responsibilities and to give another layer of comrades the chance to go in.

We can't keep putting more comrades in and taking no one out; it won't work that way. The experience of being in industry is extremely valuable. If you then take some time away from work to become organizer of a branch or take a national assignment, you understand a lot better what we're doing, what we're trying to accomplish.

National cadre school

On the question of Sandstone University. This is a big project. It's going to take a lot of resources that we do not yet have. It's going to take leadership adjustments. Even if each class is only eight or ten comrades, each one of them is today doing something important and we'll have to juggle a lot of assignments.

We all agree that we must do this if we are going to collectively prepare ourselves and meet the challenge we face. But it's an exciting prospect and we are convinced that the entire party will respond enthusiastically. We think the resources to do it are there. But we should think about it as a collective responsibility of the leadership. If we really want this school, we have to organize to make sure that it can happen.

We should also be very conscious that it's not going to solve the general educational problems of the party. It will help to educate the entire party but it's not a substitute for our general education program. It's not a substitute for the weekly branch educationals, politically thought-out branch meetings, new members classes, weekend class series, summer schools, and other branch, local, and district educational activities. It's not a substitute for taking the time to talk politics with comrades, get them interested in reading the classics, and help them relate their experiences to our overall political strategy.

It's no substitute, but it will make all of these challenges easier to meet. And it will raise the consciousness of the entire party on this vital question of constantly renewing and enriching our understanding of Marxist politics.

The school will start with members of the elected national leadership, the National Committee. That's where we have to begin. That will help to push us all forward.

Preparing the convention

A couple of comrades asked about the preparations for the election of the National Committee at the convention. We should urge comrades to read the February 1978 plenum report, and this one prior to the convention.

The leadership questions we dealt with here and in the turn report are things the delegations should discuss prior to the convention as they think about nominations for the National Committee, and think about which comrades should be asked to serve on the nominations commission.

Comrades raised a couple of concerns after the last convention. The nominating commission felt there had not been adequate discussion in the delegations themselves prior to the convention about the nominations to be made. And they thought more consideration should be given to who went on the nominating commission from each delegation. It's a difficult assignment. It's tiring and members of the commission sometimes miss some convention sessions. There's frequently a reluctance to serve on the commission more than once.

But it's one of the most important assignments, one of the most important responsibilities at the convention. It must have a good number of comrades with previous experience on the commission, comrades whose judgement everyone respects. So, leadership attention should be given to thinking out who goes on the nominating commission from your delegation.

A historic opportunity

The leadership challenges we're talking about are not basically conjunctural questions. They're real historical challenges. They're not things you resolve overnight or that you leap over in an ahistorical act of will. It's not being pessimistic to say that. That doesn't mean there is nothing we can do to effect changes. We *can* move forward in a fundamental way, if we are honest about the real challenge.

But we shouldn't think that if we get everybody into industry, we're going to solve all leadership questions overnight.

What is new, what is different, is that the kind of transformation the entire party is going through gives us a new and positive framework in which to address ourselves to these questions. That will maximize our ability to deal objectively with the challenges we face and move forward in the political development of the entire leadership of the party.

That is a very optimistic perspective.

LEADING THE PARTY INTO INDUSTRY
Excerpt from report adopted by SWP National Committee, February 1978

by Jack Barnes

What is the leadership of this kind of party like? We have a new, large (the largest in the history of the party) relatively young National Committee. But it has one of the biggest responsibilities and maybe the biggest opportunity of any national leadership of the history of the party. So we wanted to take a little time on this part of the report to discuss this question of questions—the question of leadership.

We have to begin by looking at what our leadership concepts are derived from. Forms, structure, and norms of leadership are derived basically from three things:

• One, the character of the revolution we are out to lead. Different kinds of leadership are necessary to lead different kinds of revolutions.

• Two, the character of the party we need once we decide the character of the revolution we are determined to lead.

• Three, the concrete stage we are at in building that party.

Our leadership needs and norms will be different at different stages in the development of the party. Let's step back and look at each of these.

The character of the revolution is no mystery to us. Its rich concreteness is; but not its essential character. We have come to agreement on this and have codified it in our resolutions. We believe that the coming American socialist revolution will have a combined character. It will be a revolution to free the working class from exploitation, to free the toiling masses from oppression. The revolution will also be a struggle for the right of self-determination of the oppressed nationalities. The Black struggle, and the struggle of the other oppressed nationalities, have great weight and importance. As Trotsky reminded us, the class-conscious workers of these nationalities will play a role as the vanguard of the proletariat.

The coming American revolution will be a combined revolution in another sense, too. The drive to achieve equality for women, to solve the problems the women's liberation movement is posing, will be one of the central motor forces of the revolution. The revolutionary mobilization of women will be decisive in defeating capitalism. The revolution will have to combine the solutions to this question with all its other tasks.

What does the revolutionary party fight for to bring this combined socialist revolution to fruition? The establishment of a workers government. A workers government must replace the current capitalist government. That workers government must get rid of the capitalist state and establish a workers state. *Not* a combined state, but a workers state. That's the only way that these combined tasks can be accomplished successfully. The bourgeoisie cannot do it. Only the proletariat can do it. Thus the combined revolution must be a workers revolution, if it is to establish a workers government. It is important not to confuse these two things—the *combined tasks* of the socialist revolution, and the *proletarian character* of the revolution that makes it possible to accomplish these tasks.

Character of the party

What can we conclude from this about the character of the party? If the party is going to lead a proletarian revolution to establish a workers state, it has to be a proletarian party. It has to be a proletarian party in program, composition, and in its experience. And it must understand and consciously relate to the epoch it is in: its task is not one of reforming capitalism, its realistic perspective is the elimination of capitalist rule.

It has a single program, not a bunch of different programs. It has what we call the transitional program. We reject any concept of sectoralism or polyvanguardism. We are opposed to any idea of a combined state, or a combined party. The way forward is that of a proletarian revolution and the vanguard has to be the organized, conscious vanguard of the proletariat.

The most powerful, centralized ruling class in history has to be displaced. But that doesn't end the matter. There's an additional important problem: the proletariat is not homogeneous. If the proletariat—who are the big majority—were totally homogeneous, if every worker went through the same experiences and came to the same conclusions at the same time, a conscious political homogeneous combat party wouldn't be so needed. You could try to slip by through utilizing the broadest class institutions—the industrial unions, councils, soviets, whatever. These are the institutions that by definition encompass the great active majority of the whole class. But in reality, just when that stage is reached—the stage of the transformation of the gigantic industrial unions into revolutionary instruments of struggle, the establishment of workers councils, the establishment of soviets—it's just at that point that the heterogeneous character of the class, based on historic differences along lines of craft, race, sex, age, and political experience—makes the need for the party so acute.

At that point a party is needed that will speak for the most conscious elements of the proletariat, and lead the fight to oppose and win the least conscious and the most backward elements, those most affected by bourgeois and petty-bourgeois ideology. It will lead the most conscious elements to take power for the class. Thus, it is not a matter of indifference whether the party is rooted in, and a significant part of its leadership as well as its membership is composed of sectors of the working class that are doubly oppressed in capitalist society. These are the workers who will be among the best fighters and the most courageous and conscious leaders of the party and of the class.

The rise of the Black struggle and the explosion of nationalist consciousness, and the rise of the women's struggle, have had a great impact, a historical impact we've often discussed. But they have one meaning above all others for the revolutionary party: the human material, the potential leaders of the proletarian party, have been increased many times. And that may be the most important meaning for us.

If this is true it says something else about the leaders of the party. They *all* lead the party, not a sector of the party or a grouping in the party. Naturally, leaders are looked to in a special way by sections of the party. Leaders who are women are looked to by younger women in the party as examples, as people to learn from. The same with Black comrades. We all go through this experience. When you find someone like yourself, with whom you can identify, it helps you have the confidence to take strides forward.

But what we are after is not Black leaders of the party, or Chicano leaders of the party, or women leaders of the party, or worker leaders of the party. What we are after is leaders of the party—rounded leaders of the party, looked to by the entire party, who are Black, Chicano, Puerto Rican, female, and workers in industry. Not Black leaders of the party, but party leaders who are Black. Not leaders who take responsibility for only one section of the party, or one area of work, but leaders who take overall responsibility, who lead the work of the entire party, and who are looked to by the entire party.

The stage we're at in building the party and the decision we're making at this plenum also has an important bearing on the leadership question. Industry is where the proletarian leadership will develop. Industry will not be the only place, because there are struggles of the oppressed occurring in other arenas also. But industry will be the major place and these struggles of the oppressed will be led by workers. It will be primarily in industry where our leaders will gain experience and confidence and come forward. This is universal, for the party as a whole.

No different roads

We do not have different roads to leadership. We cannot have different roads, for white and Black, male and female, more and less experienced cadres. We cannot have different roads or it simply won't work. Our work in industry, and getting into industry, is the central responsibility of the party. It is the central leadership responsibility of all cadres. This is where the next leadership of the proletarian party historically, and the leaders of the next stage of the mass movement, will be found. It is true not only for the future class-struggle left wing in the unions, but for the Black movement, the Chicano movement, the Puerto Rican movement, the women's movement. It's from here and not from the ranks of lawyers, preachers, professors, labor fakers, petty-bourgeois politicians, and ex–government officials that the leaders of the Black movement, the women's movement, will come. They are going to be found among the American working class and that is where we have to go and get them.

There is another side to this, too. In thinking about this report I went back and read *The Struggle for a Proletarian Party*. I was struck by something that I hadn't remembered so much from earlier readings: the stress that Jim put on *attitudes* toward leadership and organization. He listed a lot of the characteristics of proletarian leaders. Seriousness toward the organization of the leadership. Objectivity. Subordinating personal considerations in putting the party first. Having a professional attitude toward it. Being deadly opposed to gossip, cynicism, bureaucratism, supersensitivity to criticism. Jim stressed that all of these traits, and more, were proletarian attitudes toward the party.

And it wasn't only Cannon's view. Trotsky's praise of *Struggle for a Proletarian Party* and his writings on organization and leadership in *In Defense of Marxism* made the same point, based on the decades of experience of the Bolsheviks. We incorporated this view as part of the fundamental program of the party. [See "The Organizational Character of the Socialist Workers Party, Resolution Adopted by the 21st National Convention of the Socialist Workers Party, September 1965," Education for Socialists Bulletin.]

Above all, *objectivity is the key to this*. To lead and set an example on the organization question, on the leadership question, above all we have to be objective and not subjective. The vantage point has to be not "me and mine" but "us and ours." The starting point has to be the needs of the party, the needs of the class.

The closed session at the convention

These general points were reflected in our last convention during the discussions in the final session. The discussion there reflected the fact that the character of the leadership is derivative from our broader political goals and stage we have reached. It also showed the objective character of the leadership/organization decisions that we have to make.

One point was the review of our marijuana policy. [See "The SWP's Security Policy on Illegal Drugs," Internal Information Bulletin No. 7 in 1977.] The delegates cold-bloodedly and objectively— subordinating any secondary factors or subjective attitudes—made a decision that in the interests of the party it was necessary to maintain this policy. This decision came easy, almost automatically once the facts were presented. And this ease is not unimportant. It showed our capacity to be objective, to put the party first, to subordinate everything to what we are trying to accomplish in the long run. The class enemy is subordinating everything to what they are trying to accomplish in the long run. They are cold-blooded as hell. We can rest assured of that.

The second point we took up was the report by Linda [Jenness] from the outgoing Political Committee, on the conclusions of the Control Commission on violence within the movement, wife-beating, and the limits to "privacy" in the proletarian party. Not only were we able to act unanimously on that, but the degree to which we were able to carry through that discussion objectively was a test of something else. It was a test of the party's determination to apply no double standards. We have no different membership requirements, no different standards, and no different responsibilities, for Black and white, male and female, industrial workers or not. If we slipped into that, we would undermine everything we have been talking about. The report approved by the convention, based on the Control Commission investigation that was conducted, was also a cold-blooded, objective policy guideline that we adopted as party law.

Thirdly, we discussed out and adopted the report that Catarino Garza gave, on exclusive social affairs. This was not minor at all. What was really being discussed was not only the mistakes that were made on what kind of social gatherings were appropriate at conventions. It wasn't too difficult to get agreement on that. But something much deeper was involved—the multinational proletarian character of the party. We had to cut through any kind of subjectivity, sectoralism, any attitude that leaders are leaders of sections of the party rather than the party in its totality. And errors like this that could unintentionally lead to cliquism. That was what was being discussed under that point and what was unanimously settled.

National Committee election
Finally we had the election of the National Committee. I can only give a personal opinion on this but I think the convention elected a good National Committee. Of course it's hard not to elect a good National Committee. The National Committee is only a small percentage of the leadership of the party, and if we can't elect a good National Committee, we would be in bad shape.

Some of the discussion we had on this point bears on the question of leadership, where we are right now in the turn, and what kind of leadership we are going to have to have. (I leave aside the fault of the outgoing national leadership in not better preparing the discussion for the convention.)

There are two points that came up in the discussion that are worth reviewing today—six months later. One is what I call the "too-many-white-males-in-the-leadership" question. The second is the purpose of the National Committee election itself, what it is supposed to accomplish.

Let's begin with the "white male question." First, we can state the obvious. We cannot lead the proletarian revolution without hundreds of thousands of white males in the party and this will be reflected also in its leadership. It's safe to assume there's agreement on this.

But something else is underneath. What's underneath is not this obvious fact that we can't have too many white males (or any other category) acting like leaders, but the attitude that the party takes on affirmative action in leadership development. Some comrades are uncomfortable with the phrase "affirmative action." I like it very much. And I don't know of any better term to use. I think we should take affirmative action to advance into the leadership of the party, in every possible way, comrades from the oppressed nationalities, female comrades, young workers who come into the party. We must say that explicitly and we must do it if what we say is true about the character of the U.S. working class, the character of the coming revolution, and the character of the party that derives from this.

We all know how the working class is divided along race and sex lines, how society is divided. The revolutionary unity of the class, within the class and with the allies of the class, must be based on championing the needs of the oppressed, not defending the privileges a thin layer gets from the oppressors. This is the only basis on which the working class can be led to victory.

A revolutionary party must reflect this fact not only in its program but in the composition of its leadership. This isn't something that can be left to nature or left to chance. It will not happen "naturally"—that is, without conscious leadership. Why not? Because part of the division of this society is what the oppressed are taught about themselves from the day they are born. Blacks, Chicanos, females, are taught in a hundred different ways that they are not leaders, they are not self-confident, they are not clear thinkers, cold-blooded decisive Leninist types. That's the idea. The schools, churches, and mass media try to structure society's consciousness that way. A party that won't pay special attention and affirmatively act in such a way that will move forward leaders and potential leaders from the oppressed is simply avoiding its responsibility.

An objective necessity
That's why I like the term affirmative action. The party must act affirmatively to advance in every way possible the development of women, Black, Chicano, and Puerto Rican comrades, and comrades recruited out of working-class struggles. We must set a framework in which this responsibility and this opportunity can be advanced. This has nothing to do with guilt or moralism or similar hypocritical mouthings that mark so many "socialist" sects. It is an objective question of whether we will be able to do what we have to do. The coming American revolution cannot be led by a party that has a sexual and racial composition—in its ranks and in its leadership—like other revolutionary parties in the past, including even the Bolsheviks. This need is dictated by the nature of the American working class, and the history of the class struggle. Anything short of the goal we have

set ourselves isn't going to be good enough for us in this country in this period.

We cannot confuse affirmative action with quotas. We are for affirmative action but we are ironclad in our rejection of quotas in the construction of the Leninist party. We are the world's experts on quotas. I don't have to explain to this plenum why we say affirmative action is a fake in industry, in education, without quotas. Quotas are the only possible way we can check the rulers, can force them to retreat. It's the only way that we can raise people's consciousness about this.

Quotas are necessary in another arena too. Quotas are needed in the workers movement. For instance, in various situations in the unions today. Why must we have affirmative action quotas in the unions? Why do we fight for the establishment of women's committees, for the right of all-Black caucuses and all-women's caucuses to function in the unions? We do it because of the program of the union bureaucracy. It is not a program in the interest of the class. And the leadership of the unions is not democratically elected to carry out a program in the interests of the class. One of the ways we can bust this down and change this is by fighting for quotas.

This is not just a question of the unions today. We will be for quotas under a workers government in the United States. We will be for quotas because the workers government will represent all the workers, not just the most conscious workers. It will be a government that will have more than one party. These different parties will represent different strata in the working class. These parties will have different programs. They will contend with each other. The coming to power of a workers government, and the establishment of a workers state, will not totally erase differentiations within the working class. Not at all. The most conscious section of the working class will still need to fight for the unity of the class through support to the interests of the most oppressed. It will still have to fight to bust through the effects of decades of misleaders of the working class and the legacy of centuries of oppression.

Program and Leninist norms

But we do not use the same criteria within the Leninist party. We must remember the differences.

The party's program is a revolutionary program. The party's leadership is democratically elected. The only way the party can function is to base every decision on *political* criteria. And the only way to keep the real leadership (in the eyes of the party) and the elected leadership the same is to function in this way. The party is the *conscious* vanguard of the class. These are the decisive elements that make the party different from the unions today, from the other mass organizations of the class, from the future soviets. Remember, we don't advocate all our Leninist organizational norms for any other organization.

So we are against quotas, against caucuses in the Leninist party. But we are for affirmative action in leadership development and advancement. We are for finding ways and means on all levels to advance party leadership experience of comrades of oppressed nationalities, women comrades, young workers. We are for maximizing the pace of that experience, and maximizing the formal decisions that reflect and encourage that experience.

But that is *not* the same as saying that we *won't* advance that leadership experience for white males (or Jews or older comrades or any other "category"). It is not the same at all. Even the way we elect leaderships proves this point. And this is important.

When we elect the National Committee, the delegates vote *for* the nominees they would like to see on the NC. They are not asked to choose whom they *don't* want on it. The mathematics of it has an important political meaning. What happens is a group of delegates, all with equal weight, democratically elected, write down on a piece of paper 83 names of people they would like to see on the National Committee. They don't write down the 10 or 50 or 1,600 names of those they don't think should be on it. This is true no matter how many nominations there are. There may be 2,000 nominations or there may be 83 nominations. The delegates write down those names, then their votes are added up, and the 83 highest vote-getters are the National Committee of the party for a year or two.

It is not the party's job to pick people *not* to be leaders or *not* to have responsibilities. It's not our job to put obstacles in anyone's way to shouldering more responsibility. To the contrary. It is true that when we elect someone to a certain responsibility we are excluding other people from having that formal responsibility at that time. But that exclusion is never our starting point.

What is the National Committee?

There is a second aspect of this question. What is the National Committee? The first thing to say is that it is a *committee*. Being an individual "NCer" doesn't really mean much—at least in the way of privileges. The only one I know of is listed in Article V, Section 3, paragraph 4 of the Constitution which says if an NCer is caught being disloyal to the party he or she can only be suspended by a two-thirds vote of the NC, losing all rights and twisting in the wind until the next convention chucks them out. Some privilege!

The "Organizational Character of the Socialist Workers Party" lists some unambiguous *responsibilities* however: ". . . Membership in the leading staff of the party, the National Committee, must be made contingent on a complete subordination of the life of the candidate to the party. All members of the National Committee must be prepared to devote full-time activities to party work at the demand of the National Committee. . . .

"The leadership of the party must be under the control of the membership, its policies must always be open to criticism, discussion and rectification by the rank and file within properly established forms and limits, and the leading bodies themselves subject to formal recall or alteration. The membership of the party has the right to demand and expect the greatest responsibility from the leaders precisely because of the position they occupy in the movement. The selection of comrades to the positions of leadership means the conferring of an extraordinary responsibility. The warrant for this position must be proved, not once, but continuously by the leadership itself. It is under obligation to set the highest example of responsibility, devotion, sacrifice and complete identification with the party itself and its daily life and action. It must display the ability to defend its policies before the membership of the party, and to defend the line of the party and the party as a whole before the working class in general."

But the National Committee *as a committee* means a great deal. When the committee meets as a committee and makes decisions as a committee, it acts as the national leadership of the party, as if the party is in the room. That's what's important.

Secondly, it's important to remind ourselves that the National Committee is not the totality of the leadership of the party. The leadership of the party is much bigger and broader than the National Committee, the Political Committee, local executive committees, or any other committees. The leadership of the party is those who lead. It's good to keep that in mind.

Leadership development

What can be accomplished in the actual election to the National Committee? The National Committee election simply reflects something that has *already taken place.* The National Committee *election* is not so important as it sometimes seems. It's not a historic event in the class struggle. The National Committee election is a way of democratically formalizing a rounded committee of eighty-three, or whatever the number is, of comrades who have already taken leadership. To be *elected* to the National Committee doesn't *make* you a national leader. Being elected to the National Committee has nothing to do per se with being a leader. Either you are a leader or are not. If the national convention recognizes it, good. If it doesn't, wait until next year.

However, if it doesn't recognize enough of the leadership over time, then we have a real problem. Then a disparity develops between the real leadership and the formal leadership. The purpose of the election of the National Committee is to recognize and formalize the reality of the party leadership.

If it did not do this, we would be in trouble. Everyone knows who the leadership of the party is. The real leadership of the party is those you go to when you have political problems, those whose opinions you listen to when important decisions are being made. Those you look to for leadership. The National Committee had damn well better be those same people, basically, or it won't have the authority and the respect of the party. That's where we should begin. Thus, there are narrow limits on what the election of the National Committee itself accomplishes in terms of affirmative action. Of course, certain things can be done. If the nominations commission and delegates are conscious of what we are trying to do—as they are—this process can be nudged forward somewhat. But that's about all.

But the heart of the process of leadership development, including affirmative action, does not occur during the election of the National Committee. Broadening and training the leadership of the party must occur in the branches, the locals, the fractions. That's where our affirmative action takes place, where the conscious leadership development takes place. That's where it happens. There we can use some guidelines. We have to be conscious of what we're doing. For one thing, we have to fight against *stereotyping* of assignments.

Another thing that we want to keep in mind is that every responsibility is a collective one. You never stick a comrade in a job and then say that comrade is over his or her head and then criticize them for it. The comrades who have given the assignment or have given the responsibility, the executive committee or the branch, are responsible for the comrade who takes it. Every assignment is collective. Every assignment must be worked on in a collective way.

Next, leadership more than anything else means taking *general* responsibility. Leaders are not those who just exert themselves in their particular assignment. Leaders are those who, in addition to their responsibility within whatever division of labor we have, are always shouldering other responsibility. They are thinking about the party as a whole, the branch as a whole, and helping.

There are obvious things the leadership can do, some affirmative action we can take, to advance the process of leadership development. One, we can explicitly encourage it and we can aid the party to do this, in every structure—from the national field organizers to the branch executive committees.

'Sandstone University'
The second thing we can do is start what Jim Cannon described as The National Full-Time Training School, popularly called the Trotsky School. (We could call it the Cannon School or Sandstone University or some other appropriate name. I like Sandstone University since the idea was developed collectively in discussions by the comrades serving the Smith Act sentences at Sandstone, Minnesota. The original proposal is reprinted in *Letters from Prison*. It's worth rereading. It also serves to remind us that we'll all probably get a chance sometime to do graduate work under similar conditions.) [See *Letters from Prison*, Pathfinder Press, 1968, 1973, pp. 108–115 (2009 printing).]

We are not ready to make this decision now. For one thing, we've got to find ways to finance it without disrupting other things. Maybe we can start a campaign to raise the money to do it. Maybe some comrades will come forward to help us finance it. But it would be irresponsible not to begin it soon.

There's a very simple law to the development of leadership, one that we have to watch. Comrades who shoulder all sorts of responsibility, who move forward and take more and more responsibility, will not automatically take the time—if they are active workers and active comrades—to step back, think, read, periodically rearm themselves politically. This is especially true for comrades who develop in the party along certain roads. I think this can be true, for example, among many women comrades. Some comrades become extremely efficient and experienced organizers. They organize branches and fractions and all kinds of things. But along the way they don't have the time, the inclination, the encouragement, or the training to arm themselves politically, thoroughly, and consistently.

We have got to get rid of any implicit idea that this is okay. That it's just going to be that way. That's baloney. We are not a party in which some *do* extremely well and some *think* extremely well and it all works out. That would be a fatal weakness of a party. The Sandstone University relates to our affirmative action. But that's not all it is. It is aimed at advancing all the cadres of the party.

Developing every comrade
As important as our special responsibility is to advance women and comrades of the oppressed nationalities, this is subordinate to and must be placed within the framework of our main job. That job is to maximize, in all ways possible, the conditions for the development of *every single member* of this party as cadres of the SWP and leaders of the proletariat, in whatever fields are open to them. That is our overriding responsibility.

There are different ways we can do this. One of the most fundamental is very simple. The leadership has to give every single comrade a fair shot. We must work with each comrade in the same way, have no favoritism, regardless of nationality, sex, age, background, or experiences. Every leader is a leader of the party. They must see themselves as a leader of the whole party. Every member of the party must have confidence in every single leader—that they will get an objective hearing, a fair shot, and working relations with them on the same footing as anyone else. This is our strength.

We don't want any Abernite-type efficiency. And we don't want any comrades thinking that they lead certain comrades but not others. We don't want a leadership that doesn't have the confidence of the entire membership. The party's elected leadership body is responsible for the work of the party as a whole and the development of all comrades. This is what we seek, and we have made important strides forward in this in the last couple of years.

Within this framework, there are all kinds of organizational norms that help. One is that committees are more important than individuals. We should think of ourselves less as directors of work and more as a fraction head or a committee chair, because this approach is more efficient and you get better ideas. Anyone who sits alone in a room can come up with ideas—often weird ideas. When you just talk to people who think exactly like you, you can get off on a tangent. When you hang around people not all like you, you get more rounded ideas. If you think your closest friends are the people you work together with best as a political team, you are going off the track.

It is useful to review the role of the executive committees and the organizer. The organizer is not the organizer of the branch or the local. The executive committee is the organizer of the branch or the local. The organizer is simply the executive officer of the executive committee. It's more important that the committee itself function well and take more and more responsibility than to have a super-efficient high-powered organizer. We don't care if we don't accomplish some task perfectly because the most experienced comrade is not assigned to it. We care about the experiences and development of the cadre as a whole.

What a good organizer can accomplish is measured in terms of how well the executive committee develops how many cadres for the next stage of leadership. Of course, this is true not just for organizers, but for work directors and fraction heads. Anyone leading anything at all is always preparing their own future replacement. What you do and what you accomplish in the short run is less important than how the party machine works after you have left for another assignment. Measure what you've accomplished by how many comrades you have made more self-confident and knowledgeable. How many you have taught by example that leaders are those who lead, and that every single comrade who does so is a leader of the party.

The second norm we should keep in mind is that leadership is how, and not what. People lead by *how* they do things, and not by *what* particular thing they do. Think of all our tasks as being accomplished by Bolshevik labor power. It's not *what* concrete form it takes that determines its value to the party. It's *how* well we all work that counts. And that's what we value.

Leaders never accept or reject a responsibility because of a post involved. They never reject responsibility because they are not on a committee. They accept general responsibility, for the success of their assignment and for everyone else's, as much as humanly possible.

Professional revolutionists

There is another aspect to this: leadership has nothing to do with being full-time. Leaders have to be ready to take full-time assignments. But all leaders have to consider themselves professional revolutionists, whether they work full-time for the party or not. No one ever got paid in the revolutionary party for leading. It has never happened. You lead, and whether you are full-time or not is irrelevant to *that* fact.

Finally, we should get rid of any mechanical conception of leadership development up a ladder. Our party is not the kind of a party where leadership begins by being a member of a branch committee. Then you become head of another committee. Then you become head of the sales committee. Then you become a candidate. Then you become an assistant organizer. Then you become branch organizer. Then you become city organizer. Then you become bishop of the archdiocese. Of course, there is a problem. That's the way the whole world works. But that's not the way this party works.

This is where the conjuncture comes in, where the colonization of industry comes in. There is no ladder like that in developing the leadership of the party. The leadership question is connected directly with making this turn. Leadership right now means, above all, leading this party into industry and shouldering the responsibility this implies on every level. We want the majority of the local and branch executive committees in industry. We want a bunch of our current organizers in industry as soon as we can replace them. We want to continue the process that we began with comrades on the National Committee, the trade-union steering committee, and the Political Committee—releasing leaders to get jobs in industry, to recognize and take advantage of the openings, to go to where the future leaders of the mass movements are, and to go where our cadres are going to come forward nationally, be trained, and be tested. This is where the conjuncture and our immediate tasks come together with the more general character of the party, the character of the revolution, and the development of the leadership.

We have stressed that this is a preparatory period. We say that we are not going into industry because we are expecting immediate conjunctural gains. We should also stress something else. If we carry this out, and get the big majority of the party into industrial unions, if the leadership leads, if the majority of the branch and local leadership lead this work, we are going to recruit. We are beginning to recruit in industry, not fast, but it will step up.

The party is going to be transformed. We will have a different milieu for our campaigns and we will recruit. This will strengthen every part of the party's work. It will strengthen us in community struggles, in NOW, in the Chicano movement, in the NAACP, in the anti-*Bakke* work, in every single campaign that we are involved in.

We should be grateful we have a preparatory period so we can use it. But we don't want to dawdle. What Trotsky said about the American workers moving with American speed wasn't just to enthuse us. It is the truth. We have no mass Stalinist party, no mass Socialist Party, no reformist labor party. We do not have a defeated working class, or a discouraged working class, no enraged petty-bourgeoisie. These obstacles do not exist. We know historically, we know as sure as we are sitting here, that the kind of crisis that we are now in—the economic crisis and the offensive of the ruling class—has always produced in this country an explosive radicalizing motion in the American working class. It is going to happen again.

This is a unique opportunity for the party in another way. We have never before decided on a shift like this, responded to an opening like this, when we didn't have to have a faction fight inside the party. We don't have an opposition in the party today. We have a party that is waiting to be led. The comrades are waiting to have presented to them what we are going to do. In the opinion of the Political Committee, that is the challenge of this plenum. It is the opportunity—and the real test—for this leadership.

FROM THE SUMMARY

The discussion showed we agree we are at a new stage in thinking through the questions relating to leadership. We can now put behind us the confusion and unthought-out criteria that marred the convention discussion on the election of the National Committee. As Matilde explained, our decision today gives us a new common framework to move forward on this question.

I just want to reemphasize what our opinion is concerning the real issues in the election of the National Committee. One concerns the role of the election of the National Committee itself. This was being exaggerated in an attempt to solve problems other than what it is supposed to solve. We need to put the actual election of the National Committee in proper perspective, and de-emphasize it as the way to solve all leadership challenges.

Secondly, at the last convention, in the closed session, we got off what has to be the axis of any NC election discussion: to make sure the convention elects the current real leadership of the party. The discussion focused on something else, on how to advance the process of bringing more nonwhite and women comrades onto the national leadership bodies of the party. The convention can give one or two nudges to this process, but the day the National Committee ceases being, above everything else, the reflection of the real leadership of the party, that is the day we start developing cliques and informal unelected leadership groupings in the party.

That was the problem with the "white male" question. That was where it was wrong. The National Committee had better include the white males who are leading this party—along with every other category—or the National Committee could over time become a joke.

There was a separate discussion that was intertwined with this. What does the party do on affirmative action—or whatever phrase you want to use. Some comrades feel it is incorrect to say we are making up for past injustice society has created. I don't think so. Society has created an *injustice* and because of that an *obstacle* has been made for the party. I don't see how it could not. Where do we recruit people from? Not from a socialist society. We recruit from this society. A society in which the working class has been divided along race, sex, and age lines. Some of it, like the oppression of women, has lasted for millennia. Some of it, like the oppression of Blacks, has occurred over centuries.

But there are also limits on what the party can do. We can be conscious, we can be open, and totally frank about the realities of the problem outside and the challenge inside the movement. We can be conscious as Leninists about what to do about it, and we can take concrete steps to become more and more conscious in advancing this process. But there finally comes a moment when you have to say what Farrell used to tell the Teamsters: take what you are big enough to take. Leadership is taken, it is not given. You take what you are big enough to take. All the party can do is to maximize the conditions for this.

Along these same lines there is one other point that Gerry raised that I want to say something about. That is avoiding a mechanical or even brutal way of carrying out our decision to rapidly get a large majority of our comrades in industry. The last thing the party would do would be to destroy the carefully built-up professionalism of the party, to tear down the apparatus of the party, including the literary and journalistic staffs, our publishing and printing operations, all the things we have worked so hard to put on a professional footing.

If we succeed in this new turn, I think history teaches us that the party will value these kinds of accomplishments, and this kind of contribution, more than ever before. We will be hungrier for the best *Militant,* hungrier for the best books, hungrier for the best *Intercontinental Press/Inprecor,* hungrier for the development of all the party institutions that we have, and must have. And hungry to integrate workers we will be recruiting onto these staffs.

And finally, above everything, we have to watch one thing: we have to evaluate the work of our various industrial fractions as much as we can on a collective nationwide level. We want to avoid anything that makes comrades in industry feel that the key is what they accomplish individually. Thabo says he talks politics eight hours a day on the job. But not everyone can do that. You may find yourself working with people whom you can't talk to at all—just like twenty years ago. I know comrades who are working in industry who are working with three people in some departments. Or sometimes you hit a little dry spot where you can't do much.

The key thing is that it's the *fraction,* not the individual, that will accomplish things. Comrades have got to feel that what we accomplish will be measured on a national level, not simply on a local level. It will be accomplished collectively, not individually. And it will be accomplished by the whole party.

The party must understand the importance of nationwide fractions in major industry. We have to have national fractions. We have one national fraction in steel. Now we have to move toward a national fraction in rail, and a national fraction in auto. And that's just the bare beginning.

Thabo says, "This is it." I agree with him. For a couple of decades now we've fought against saying, "This is it." One of the biggest problems the party had was people deciding prematurely that the time was right to throw ourselves into industry.

But now the time is right.

VIOLENCE AGAINST WOMEN IS INCOMPATIBLE WITH PARTY MEMBERSHIP

Excerpt from 'Political Committee report on Control Commission recommendations,' report adopted by SWP National Convention, August 13, 1977

by Linda Jenness

During the last year, the Political Committee has taken action on three recommendations from the Control Commission. Two of these recommendations involved cases of violence in the movement and the third involved a review of our security policy on the use of illegal drugs and marijuana.

This report is not a report from the Control Commission. It is a report from the Political Committee to the convention on some general conclusions on membership norms the party must enforce. These are conclusions that we came to in the course of discussing these specific cases.

This report is in two parts. The first part concerns violence in the movement. The second regards our security policy on drugs.

Comrades have in their delegates' kits the reports from the Control Commission on its investigations involving two cases of violence by one comrade against another. The individuals in both cases have resigned from the party and there are no formal proposals for discipline or appeals before us. The purpose of this report is not to review these cases, but to summarize the conclusions on membership norms reached by the Political Committee as a result of the cases.

The conclusions that we are presenting here are not new. They do not deal with acts that were previously condoned by our movement and that we now condemn. Rather, they represent a more explicit and more clearly defined explanation of what we mean when we say that violence within the movement is incompatible with membership in the Socialist Workers Party.

In investigating the two cases of violence, the Control Commission found that some comrades, who had not had to deal with and think out this question before, had too narrow a view of what is included. It was in helping these comrades think out that question that the Political Committee divided the question of unacceptable violence in the movement into four categories.

The first category is undisciplined free-lancing in combat situations. We have the task of organizing the revolutionary combat party that must lead the workers to take power from the ruling class in the United States. We need to construct a combat party that can lead the workers to defeat the ultimate violence—that is, the fascist gangs that will be unleashed on our class by the most vicious and most powerful ruling class in history.

We understand the need for discipline in class battles. Any free-lancing, including in self-defense initiatives, would be disastrous. If members took it upon themselves to decide individually when to handle scabs, or defend the workers movement against police attack, if they were not disciplined when marshaling a demonstration, or in organizing defense against the violence of the ultraright— the combat discipline needed would break down.

The working class cannot defeat the ultraright or defend ourselves against the cops through individual acts. It takes organized, collective power that is *politically* guided. For the revolutionary party to permit its members to act in an undisciplined, individual fashion would not only endanger the party but would miseducate workers and the oppressed nationalities on this key question.

The second category is the use of violence to settle differences or disagreements in the party. Any kind of violence between comrades totally cuts across democratic discussion and the frank and open exchange of ideas—the bedrock of a disciplined party. We are a democratic-centralist organization, meaning democracy within the party in reaching decisions and centralism and discipline in action. If physical intimidation is introduced among comrades, democracy becomes meaningless. You can't have a democratic discussion if you think someone is going to punch you out if you disagree with them. Intimidation, not encouragement to discuss, becomes a creeping cancer. It ultimately destroys confidence in each other and in the party, and decisions are not arrived at democratically.

Use of any form of violence in the party to settle disputes would also open up the party and its members to victimization, frame-up, and police provocation. It would give agents and informers a beautiful handle. We should remember the tragic case of the police-inspired feud between the Black Panther Party and Ron Karenga's US organization, and other similar examples.

There is seldom any confusion about the use of violence to settle political differences, but what happens when we are dealing with personal situations between comrades? This is the third category—the use of violence between comrades in a personal or "family" framework.

The Control Commission reported to the Political Committee that some comrades thought violence "within the family"—say, between two comrades who live together—was an exception to our policy against violence within the movement. Maybe, some comrades thought, that's just a personal matter, a private affair, and not the business of the party.

In the discussions we had in the Political Committee about this, it became clear to us that violence between comrades was never just a "personal matter." Any violence between comrades, whether over personal or political matters, introduces physical intimidation and undermines party democracy. If you feel safe on the branch floor, but think that under the guise of a "personal or private" matter you might get the stuffing beat out of you at home—your democratic rights are not exactly being protected.

But, is violence between comrades at home, in private, beyond the pale of party concern? We have a long-established norm in our party that the party doesn't snoop or pry into the personal lives of comrades. The party doesn't try to dictate the hobbies, forms of relaxation, or dress of comrades. It doesn't tell people who to be friends with, or who to live with or not live with. This is a norm jealously protected, I'm sure, by the entire membership.

The Political Committee thought it important to make it crystal clear that enforcing the proscription against violence between comrades in "personal" or "private" matters as incompatible with membership is not a step back from our norm of not interfering in the personal lives of comrades.

In fact, over the past decade, if anything, the party has moved in the opposite direction. Because of the youth radicalization, the rise of Black nationalism, the women's liberation movement, and the gay liberation movement, there has been an acceleration of changing attitudes in the working class as a whole. The party, too, has been affected. There's never been less pressure than today for the party to stick its nose in comrades' private and personal affairs.

Of course, joining the party in and of itself affects your whole life. To belong to the party, for instance, you have to pay dues—that affects the amount of money you have for your personal life. You have to actively build the party—that affects the amount of time you have for your personal life. Loyalty to the party means you can't violate party decisions—like our security policy—even in the privacy of your own home.

The rule against violence—in the same way— has nothing to do with snooping into comrades' personal lives. It is protecting and defending the democratic rights of party members.

The fourth category examined by the Political Committee is the use of violence by men against women, including wife-beating, which has almost epidemic proportions in capitalist society as a whole.

Beating up on women—whether the woman is a wife, a companion, whether she is in the party or not, whether in public or in private, is incompatible with membership in the Socialist Workers Party.

The increasing consciousness of women about this issue, a product of the women's movement, has, in the last few years, brought this issue into public prominence. And there's growing consciousness that wife-beating is one of the most brutal, and yet widespread, forms of the sexist treatment of women. It is one of the clearest examples of the brutalization fostered in society by this rotten, exploitative, oppressive, class-divided system.

How would it look in the women's movement if

the party said that "comrade x is a fine comrade, a party builder, and a supporter of our program—the fact that he goes home and beats his wife up is no concern of ours"?

The principle is simple and obvious if we think about it. The actions of our members cannot be so at variance with our program and what we are fighting for that it would make the party look hypocritical or cynical to the class whose confidence we must have in the titanic battles ahead. We cannot say one thing and do another and expect ever to win the confidence of this class.

We cannot fight for the liberation of women on the one hand, and allow a member of the party to hit his female companion on the other. Workers would say—and correctly so—that our program was not worth the paper it is written on.

As I said earlier, these positions are not new. These acts were never condoned by the party. But real experience in the party this year made us think through and clarify this question. It seemed clear to the Political Committee that this would have educational value the party would appreciate; and thus we wanted to put before the delegates for their approval our codification of the fact that:

1. undisciplined free-lancing in combat situations;

2. the use of violence to settle any kind of disagreements within the movement;

3. the use of violence between comrades even in a personal or "family" situation; and

4. any use of violence by men against women—are all incompatible with membership in our party.

COMMUNIST NORMS AND NONEXCLUSIVE SOCIAL AFFAIRS
Report adopted by SWP National Convention, August 13, 1977

by Catarino Garza

The outgoing Political Committee has discussed a problem that surfaced at the convention that should be brought to the attention of the delegates, discussed, and leadership action taken.

Since it happened here and news about it will spread throughout our movement, we are bringing it before the highest body of the party, its national convention, so that we can act on it. We think it is a political problem on which educational work must be done.

It began innocently on Monday night when comrades from Latin America and Spain, and Spanish-speaking comrades from the United States, met in a Dascomb Hall lounge. Some comrades from Latin America who had never attended an SWP convention and met so many other comrades from Latin America before, thought it would be useful to organize an informal meeting of Spanish-speaking comrades. They asked other Spanish-speaking comrades to attend and many thought it was a good idea.

The meeting was held during the time allotted for recreation at the cabaret or movies. When the meeting was called to order, it turned out that about thirty or forty people were present. However, the convenors of the meeting had no agenda and had not thought how the meeting should proceed. It was finally proposed that I chair the meeting and I suggested that we hear reports from the different groups present, that we try to keep the reports down to ten minutes, and after the reports we have questions and discussion.

The meeting heard reports from Santo Domingo, Puerto Rico, Colombia, Mexico, Martinique, Spain, Costa Rica, the Latin American community in Israel, and La Raza Unida Party. The reports lasted until almost midnight. Before the meeting adjourned I made the observation to the comrades present that it was like having a conference within a convention. We announced the convention panels on Spain, Mexico, and Puerto Rico for Wednesday and the meeting broke up. Most new comrades felt they had learned something. Some comrades with more experience felt that anyone who follows *Intercontinental Press, Perspectiva Mundial,* and the press of other sections would not have learned anything new. But comrades had been able to exchange addresses, get to know each other personally, and then have follow-up conversations.

Although the meeting was held without any regrettable incidents, this was due in large part to the positive fusion atmosphere in the air. At previous conventions, for instance, such "informal" meetings were used by supporters of Comrade Moreno to begin their underground attack on the leadership of the SWP. They began by calling us racists and gringos, and their attack is now public in a book on Angola in which Moreno accuses Tony Thomas of being a traitor to his race because of the party's position on Angola. [*Angola-La Revolución Negra en Marcha,* p. 23.] In the future another "informal" meeting of this kind could be used as an arena by someone or some tendency with a particular ax to grind.

A real problem soon grew. I was invited to attend what I thought was to be a social affair of Black and Latino comrades on Wednesday. I have always enjoyed parties and said, sure, my companion and I would be there. My companion is neither Black nor Latina. One of the comrades who invited me indicated that it might not be cool if she attended. Since it was presented as a social affair I didn't think I'd enjoy myself as much as I would at some other social where my companion could also be present and said so.

I should have pressed the matter further. I didn't. That was a mistake.

The social affair was set for Wednesday. But at the meeting of Spanish-speaking comrades on Monday there was an incident that foreshadowed the problems we would encounter on Wednesday. Apparently some individual comrade at the Monday meeting had taken it upon him or herself to tell some comrades that they were not welcome at the meeting. The convenors did not know this. I as the chair did not know this. And the overwhelming majority of the comrades present did not know this. Certainly none of the comrades from Latin America knew about it.

I only found out about it later, when I was asked to prepare this report and began to gather information from delegates and visitors to our convention. The same thing happened on Wednesday night. Comrades of our party and of other Trotskyist parties were "invited" to leave the Black and Latino social on Wednesday night by some comrades of the SWP. This was done without any discussion or decision by the convention, the Presiding Committee, or the comrades assigned to plan and organize the official functions during the convention.

Among the comrades asked to leave this affair was a comrade of the Mexican Partido Revolucionario de los Trabajadores, because he originally came from the United States and is white. He was called a "gringo" by a comrade of the SWP. This is particularly offensive because "gringo" means not just Yankee; it also means stranger, invader. Imagine, a comrade from another section called an invader at a function held at our convention!

This caused some Israeli comrades who had been exiled from Argentina to protest. And it led to the comrades of the Mexican PRT, the Israeli comrades, and some other comrades leaving. They strongly protested the uncomradely treatment of the PRT member.

Another incident at the Wednesday night party involved some Asian-American comrades. One of them is not a party member, but she is married to an SWP comrade who is white, and he was asked to leave. It reached the point where an SWP member was going around the room asking people what their race was and asking people, as it was put, "to respect the feelings of nonwhite comrades by leaving the social."

You heard me correctly. Leninists at a large social affair at this convention went around telling workers of one race that the only way they could "respect the feelings" of other comrades was to get out of the social affair. These are people who in theory are going to go into combat side by side—not necessarily as friends but as comrades in arms who may have to entrust their very lives to each other.

There was even a sign on the door which stated, "Third World Comrades Only!"

Whoever it was that took it upon themselves to exclude some comrades from this party never asked the other Black, Hispanic, or Asian comrades of the SWP how they felt on this question.

The organizers of the social affair called me out of the session Thursday to explain what had happened. The initiators of the affair had looked upon it as primarily a way of getting Black and Latino comrades together, to introduce new Black, Latino, and Asian comrades to party veterans, and to help bring them closer to the party in a relaxed social atmosphere.

The comrades who organized the social affair are serious, leading comrades of the party. They were involved in workshops on Wednesday evening and arrived at the social affair after it had begun and after these incidents took place. As soon as they learned about what had happened, they and other comrades present tried to undo the damage that was done. They sought out the comrades who had been made unwelcome and some of them returned to the social affair. However, they were not successful in all cases and some new Latino comrades from branches in the South and Southwest who saw this were angered and disoriented by the attitudes toward white comrades in their branches displayed by other Latino and Black comrades.

In discussing this problem with Willie Mae Reid, she pointed out to me that regardless of the intentions of comrades who organize convention parties that exclude white comrades, such actions create a problem. She pointed out that the same argument could be made with just as much validity for all-women's social affairs at conventions because male comrades sometimes make women comrades feel uncomfortable. She explained that this argument is sometimes used by advocates of all-women's parties. But if we make it a practice for one group within the party to have its own social affairs under what appear to be party auspices, official or unofficial, we miseducate the entire party. To do that would defeat the purpose of our convention and its role in forging the multinational party we need to lead the socialist revolution in this country. That could take place in many ways.

Some of the things that we do at our convention, for example, become the standard for the way things are done in branches throughout the country. We could have branches permitting or organizing social events of this nature on the basis that it was permitted at the national convention and therefore it must be all right. That is not the case. Organizing socials like the one on Wednesday sets into motion a dynamic of its own that cuts across our main objective, the formation of the kind of party we need.

This is a problem that is going to come up at each convention as we continue to grow and to bring into our party more people of the oppressed nationalities in the United States. Capitalist society divides us, by sex, color, national origin, affectional preference, and in many other ways. In the capitalist world we seek to protect ourselves in many different ways. We have Black, Hispanic, and Asian societies, caucuses, different types of clubs, etc.

The party exists in the capitalist world and reflects the pressures society places on us as individuals and as an organization. But the party is not the capitalist world. We *combat* these pressures by conscious effort, but it is an unending pressure. Short of the revolution, and even after the bourgeoisie is replaced, there will be vestiges of capitalist training.

Our only recourse is to consciously fight those prejudices that capitalism creates in each of us.

That doesn't mean that all of us as individuals can totally overcome these problems. The party recognizes this and has no rules about who you invite to your home, except obvious categories like fascists and cops. The party doesn't say what kind of music you may listen to, whom you may live with or may not live with, etc. Those are personal relations that the party keeps its nose out of.

What the party can't tolerate is the injection of anti-internationalist conduct into the party or into any of its activities that tend to divide the party along the lines that capitalist society divides our class. It would be disastrous for our purpose.

The question is not new. In Trotsky's *History of the Russian Revolution,* in the section entitled "The Problem of Nationalities," he clearly points out that the party of the Bolsheviks, Lenin's party, never permitted itself to let national feelings cut across the central task of forging the instrument of the revolution, the multinational working-class combat party.

We know that no party in history has understood the problem of oppressed nationalities better than the Bolsheviks. They are our model. They won the support of the oppressed people of the prison house of nations that was Russia by their ceaseless fight for the rights of the oppressed people. However, no party was a more solid fighting unit of the *working class* than the Bolsheviks.

That's what we're trying to create. People who come to our movement must be trained in that internationalist proletarian tradition if they are to become revolutionists equal to history's tasks. That process is long and hard and we must patiently explain to all comrades where divisions come from. We must also make it plain that we won't tolerate any activity that weakens or divides us.

We seek to be a model to other sections of the international in this respect, and we must admit that at this convention we haven't lived up 100 percent to our own standards. That is why we are making this report to you, so that we can begin correcting this mistake. If this report is accepted, the report will be part of the official convention record and comrades throughout the world will read it. There will be no misunderstanding about our position. But more is involved than hurting the feelings of guests here or from abroad. It is a political question and thus a responsibility of the leadership to educate future party cadre.

And this is, above all, a question for the leadership of the party to handle, to lead on. The problems here were not simply the result of new comrades acting out of inexperience. If that were all that was involved, the question would be simple. But the newer comrades and contacts were following the lead of more experienced comrades, and that is where we have to begin the process of straightening this out. That is why we are bringing this report before the convention delegates for discussion and your action.

We propose that no more affairs like the one that took place here on Wednesday, or that excludes any comrade, be organized at our conventions or in the branches.

This is, of course, different from cases where the branch sometimes organizes dinners or other gatherings and assigns certain comrades to attend—for example, a dinner with contacts from NOW, or NSCAR, or the anti-nuclear-power movement, or some other political arena. Naturally comrades interested in or active in these areas of party activity would be the ones to attend.

Such affairs are completely within the normal framework of party activity. What happened here at the convention, however, is not. It cuts across our objectives and similar events do the same. That is why we propose that such "social" affairs cease.

Harry Wicks, Jim Cannon's early comrade in arms in the fight for Trotsky's program, told us earlier at this convention how in Moscow when the Fosterites met and spoke about Jim Cannon, they reminded themselves that "the son of a bitch" was a hell of an organizer.

Comrade Wicks also pointed out that the Fosterites missed the point. That what was really at the bottom of this attribute was Cannon's profound internationalism. That's how this party was begun and it remains our bedrock foundation. Any form of racism or chauvinism among SWP members is a mortal danger to the party. Among comrades, expressions like gringo, whitey, Jew when you really mean kike, can lead to spick, bitch, or nigger. That cancer is a malignancy that we will remove before it spreads. We will maintain our internationalist tradition and build the American Bolshevik party, the Socialist Workers Party.

SUMMARY

This has been a very rich discussion with a wide range of views and experiences expressed. We will incorporate key points from the discussion into the summary and publish it and the report for the entire membership to read and consider.

Several comrades raised questions about what activities the report implies that party members should not engage in. So I think that first of all it's important to clarify what the report does *not* mean.

The purpose of the report is not to suggest that comrades cannot have parties or dinners at their homes or apartments or in their rooms at conventions, and invite whomever they choose. Within the party comrades find friends and socialize with them, and whomever they invite to their homes or socialize with is their business.

Furthermore, the report was not directed to the problems of how to organize better social activities at our conventions. It is clear from the discussion that these activities need to be reexamined, reorganized, and made more attractive for everybody that comes here. We must continue the process we started a couple of years ago of drawing more Black and Latino comrades into the planning and organization of these activities.

Nor was the report suggesting that branches should not organize informal affairs with contacts that are specifically designed to help win them to the party. Sometimes those assigned to attend such gatherings will only be comrades who are involved in or knowledgeable about the area of work the contacts are interested in. In other cases, however, the contacts may be more interested in meeting people involved in *other* areas of work. Auto workers who want to find out more about the SWP won't just want to talk to other auto workers. They will want to meet comrades involved in women's liberation work, South Africa work, our election campaigns, and so on. If they are attracted to the *party*, they are not just interested in a particular arena of work, and they will want to know who else is in the party beside the kind of people they have already met.

These are questions of tactics and judgment that must be left to the branches and locals to work out.

The report concentrated on the *political* problems posed by the type of affairs held Wednesday night at this convention.

As Derrick and Hattie pointed out, regardless of the intentions of the organizers of the affair Wednesday night, the affair turned out to have negative consequences.

The real problem with events such as the Wednesday night "Third World" party was explained by several comrades. That is that they tend to become political gatherings where serious questions are taken up, but in a framework that prevents them from coming before party bodies that can resolve them. The particular section of the membership that gets invited to these affairs and therefore can participate in these political discussions is powerless to make any decisions. That can only be done by the party membership as a whole, or through democratically elected leadership bodies. Thus there is a frustration built into these meetings: a pressure to become sterile gripe sessions.

Willie Mae pointed out another aspect of this. Discussions—and pressure—about how Black comrades, or women comrades, should organize their social and even private lives often occur at such events. This kind of pressure about how comrades should lead their personal lives has no place in this party.

Hattie pointed out also that "social" affairs where Black comrades cannot bring white companions can lead to frictions not only between Black and white comrades, but also among Black comrades. They tend to divide, rather than unite, the party.

Mike related the plans for a gay men's and lesbians' party that was to have taken place during the convention. The organizers were convinced to call it off following Wednesday night's party. This particular affair clearly had a political purpose behind it. For example, Mike explained that as a supporter of the party's line on gay liberation, he was not invited, but that a comrade who isn't gay but opposes the majority's position on gay liberation was invited because he had a car and could get liquor for the party. I totally agree with Mike that it's utopian and naïve for comrades to think that political discussions do not happen at these kinds of exclusive gatherings. It's inherent in the character of such affairs that this will occur. Certain comrades are implicitly excluded on a political basis.

The logic of permitting these functions to occur could lead to a conception that there are questions of party policy that gays should discuss by themselves, that women should discuss by themselves, that Latinos should discuss by themselves, and that Blacks should discuss by themselves. It is true that in the mass movement, our comrades, when it is politically correct, participate in various caucuses—Black caucuses, women's caucuses, minority women's caucuses, etc., in order to help advance the struggle of especially oppressed sectors of the working class against the class-collaborationist domination of our class. And we defend the right of women, of Blacks, to have their own organizations, their own caucuses in the unions, on campus, etc.

But our conception of building the revolutionary party is totally different. We do not view the party as a coordinating committee of the leaderships of each sector of the mass movement. Our party is not composed of caucuses or caucus-like formations struggling for their "rights" in the party.

We are a centralized combat party and are attempting to forge a special type of instrument— the kind of organization that, as Willie Mae said, people are totally unaccustomed to when they join. Party members must have confidence and mutual trust in each other if they are going to go into battle together. And the democratically elected bodies of the party make all appropriate political decisions.

Here, I think Derrick's reference to Lenin's writings on the revolutionary party and the national question are well taken. Derrick pointed out that Lenin's view was that we cannot allow the racism and hostility that exists toward the oppressed nationalities on the part of the oppressor nationality to be expressed in the party; nor can we allow the hostility that exists for the oppressor nationality by the oppressed nationalities to divide the party.

In a centralized multinational party, the place to organize discussion of political policy is in meetings of the appropriate bodies—executive committees, fractions, national and local conventions, National Committee, and so forth.

Another danger of exclusive functions is that they can breed cliquism. As Hattie explained, when you're left out of a gathering of comrades whom you like and want to socialize with because it excludes other people you want to be with, an atmosphere is created that you're not part of the "in group"—that you're not "nationalist" enough or "feminist" enough to be part of it. This is the breeding ground of cliquism.

I raise these points not because I think there is a big problem of polyvanguardism and cliquism in the party. Rather I wanted to summarize some of the very real political dangers to the party comrades have correctly pointed to with exclusive social events.

RACE-BAITING AND COMMUNIST LEADERSHIP
Report adopted by SWP National Committee, February 1986
by Mac Warren

At the August 1985 party convention, during the session at which the National Committee was elected, a delegate from the Northern California Bay Area—who had served on the Nominations Committee and had been nominated by it for the new National Committee—took the floor to express disagreement with the Nominations Committee proposals in relation to two members of the Chicago branch. This delegate was sharply critical of the fact that one Chicago comrade, a Chicano who had previously been a member of the National Committee, was not nominated and that another Chicago comrade, who is Black and had previously been elected a regular member of the National Committee, was nominated this time as an alternate member.

On the basis of these facts, the delegate asserted that what was involved was a "rotten" situation in Chicago, in which comrades who are Black or Chicano are not getting a fair shake because of racial prejudice in the branch leadership.

No more serious accusation could be raised. If true, the charge would require immediate action by the party leadership to make sure the functioning of the branch changed, or, if that proved impossible, to expel the offenders. If false, however, it would also require immediate action—to put a halt to race-baiting in the party.

Race-baiting involves accusing comrades with whom you have a political or organizational disagreement of racial prejudice. It is an attempt to discredit their positions rather than debating them objectively. It involves calling into doubt comrades' motives or character, rather than arguing for or against a proposal on its merits.

Race-baiting is a deadly poison in the party. It makes objective political discussion impossible. It disrupts the functioning of a communist vanguard because it undermines the process of uniting in a centralized proletarian party, by means of voluntary class discipline, workers of different nationalities. Above all, it is an obstacle to advancing the construction of an inclusive leadership, objectively selected, in which the party as a whole can have confidence that each member of the leadership will treat the membership of the party in an undifferentiated way.

Immediately following the convention, the National Committee instructed the Political Committee to find out the facts, take any action necessary to deal with the situation, and to report to the next meeting of the National Committee on what it found, what it did, and, if necessary, what further steps it proposed. The Political Committee assigned me to go to Chicago to see what evidence—if any—existed to substantiate the accusation that the Chicago leadership had put obstacles in the way of Black and Chicano members of the party. If there was none, I was to investigate whether these kinds of charges were undermining objective political relations in the party and were an obstacle to the process of building the kind of leadership we have been making progress on and are determined to continue.

Following this I was assigned by the Political Committee to go to the Bay Area to report to the comrades there on the facts in Chicago. I was also to pursue the possibility that the accusations concerning Chicago—if false—could be an indication of a mode of functioning in the Bay Area itself that had to be changed.

I went to Chicago shortly after the convention. Over a period of more than a week, I met with the executive committee and individual members of the branch and then gave a report to a branch meeting. I asked all comrades for any information that would demonstrate acts of racial prejudice in any way.

Not a single comrade, in any of the meetings I attended or in any of the individual conversations I held, reported anything that could even remotely be taken as evidence that the branch leadership, or the branch as a whole, or any member of the branch, was placing obstacles in the road of the comrades who are Black, Chicano, Puerto Rican, or Asian. I found no evidence of a double standard— one for comrades who are white and another tougher one for other comrades. I should add that the comrades in Chicago impressed on me that they wanted this fact reported to the party because of the accusations that had been raised against them at the convention.

What did I find in Chicago? Several comrades expressed the opinion that racial prejudice in the branch put barriers in the way of comrades of the oppressed nationalities. But when I asked for evidence of this, what they reported did not substantiate the charge. Instead it reflected views about norms of functioning in a communist workers' party that are dead wrong.

The first thing a couple of comrades pointed to was the convention election of the National Committee—the same charge that had been raised at the convention itself. The comrades who raised this disagreed with the nominations made by the branch delegation as well as with the decision of the convention itself. They thought that the comrade who is Chicano and was previously a member of the National Committee should have been elected to the National Committee at this convention. And they thought that the comrade who is Black and who was previously a regular member of the National Committee should have been elected by the convention as a regular member, not an alternate member.

I pressed these comrades for any evidence that these decisions were results of racial prejudice. Had there been any statement indicating that these choices were prejudiced ones? Had some action been taken—openly or not—showing racial prejudice? Was there something more than just the fact of how the election to the National Committee came out? Once posed this way, it quickly became clear that there was no evidence of racial prejudice. Not *any*. There was nothing involved other than a difference of opinion over who should be elected to the National Committee, followed by the accusation of racial prejudice because the party voted differently than an individual wanted.

The second example offered by several comrades as evidence of racial prejudice was the fact that the three regular delegates to the convention elected by the Chicago branch last summer were comrades who are white. (Two of the three alternates were comrades who are Black.) I asked again, what evidence is there that there was race prejudice involved? None was offered. The fact of how the election came out—different from how some individuals wanted it—was supposed to be, in itself, the evidence.

I explained to the comrades that if there was any action taken or any statement made that they could cite to substantiate the charge that racial prejudice was involved in either of these cases, I would immediately take it to the Political Committee and urge, if the facts were proven, that corrective action be taken. But they agreed that there really was no such evidence.

The comrades who raised these points had disagreed with the decisions of the branch on who its delegates should be. They had disagreed with the branch delegation on who should be nominated for the National Committee. They had disagreed with the decision of the convention on who should be elected to the National Committee. That's all. They disagreed. That is their privilege—and we are not going to get into whether or not they were "right" or "wrong." There is no "right" or "wrong" on elections: only individual opinions, individual votes, and the results. But what they cannot do is charge, when their view is not the same as the outcome of a democratic election, that the election is evidence of racism.

It became clear in the course of the discussions in Chicago that some of the newer comrades had drawn their conclusion that racial prejudice was involved from the example set by more experienced comrades, who should have known better. It seemed to be okay—in order to try to get the party to elect the comrades you wanted elected or to assign the comrades you wanted assigned to do something—to raise accusations of racial prejudice to intimidate those who may not agree with you. Race-baiting seemed to be an acceptable mode of functioning in the party.

The charges of racial prejudice were seldom or never expressed openly in the bodies and elected committees of the party. Instead, like all other gossip, these charges were heard most often in the corridors or at social gatherings. Party members who argued privately that comrades who are Black or Chicano weren't getting even-handed treatment never raised this in the branch or in the executive committee, where it could have been discussed and action taken, if necessary. Either they didn't take their own accusations seriously, or—what would be even worse—they didn't take the party itself seriously.

Under these conditions the functioning of the branch and its leadership bodies was weakened. Insinuations about the motives of other comrades on the executive committee made objective functioning in the elected leadership virtually impossible. There was less and less discussion of objective problems and challenges in the executive committee. More and more discussions took place outside the elected committees.

The comrades who felt that such-and-such a person should be elected a delegate, or nominated for the National Committee, didn't try to argue for their proposal in an objective way. They didn't try to persuade other branch members that their nominee was the best proposal for the party. Instead, they abandoned the political discussion.

One of the comrades in Chicago, who is Black, asked me, "What does this policy on race-baiting mean? Does it mean I can't refer affectionately to other comrades as 'white boys'?" I told him yes, precisely, that's part of what it means. It is demeaning to all comrades involved for this to occur in the party. Usually the comrade who is a target of this type of "affection" doesn't appreciate it.

This is crude race-baiting. But it is not the major form race-baiting takes in the party. To focus on the cruder things like this is to miss the more frequent, and more subtle, forms of race-baiting that take place in the party.

Race-baiting is often justified on the grounds of "concern" for the development of leaders who are from the oppressed nationalities. But, of course, that is the last thing it has anything to do with.

For one thing, such "concern" over who supposedly isn't getting a fair shake in the party isn't evenhanded. In Chicago, it turns out that only some comrades of the oppressed nationalities were objects of special "concern." Many others weren't mentioned at all, including those who some comrades may feel are equally or even better qualified than others to take on additional leadership responsibilities.

More importantly, race-baiting of any kind is an *obstacle* to objectively taking every step possible to encourage the development of party leaders from the oppressed nationalities. It gets in the way of the development of comrades of the oppressed nationalities into leaders *of the party,* not just leaders of other comrades (*some* other comrades) who are Black, Puerto Rican, Chicano, *mexicano,* or Asian.

What had allowed this situation to develop in Chicago was not primarily some general weakness in the membership. It was a *default in leadership.* Experienced comrades who are Black or Chicano were in a position to call a halt to this race-baiting—and only they could ultimately do it most effectively—but they didn't do so. Some even participated in it. Most of the individual comrades who got caught up in this mode of functioning are white. They used race-baiting to try to influence the advancement of their friends in the party (and of course ultimately themselves as part of an entourage). But this could not have continued if the leading comrades, especially those who are Black or Latino, had exercised their leadership responsibilities and put a stop to it.

There is another side to the leadership default. Many comrades in Chicago thought the race-baiting was wrong. In fact, the refusal of the Chicago branch to allow the race-baiting to determine its decisions was the key thing that eventually forced this situation into the open, making it possible to deal with it. This is a measure of the strength of the Chicago branch and its leadership.

But, looking back on the situation, following the initial discussions while I was in Chicago, the comrades there concluded that they had been too slow to deal with it. Some of the comrades explained that they had earlier thought that to challenge race-baiting would be to cut across the party's political position on the national question itself. They now see how dead wrong this was. Nationalism of the oppressed nationalities is progressive in the United States today. But racial prejudices held by members of the oppressed nationalities—whether toward other oppressed nationalities, toward Jews, or toward whites in general—are not progressive in any sense. They are reactionary.

Unclarity on this is a danger for the party. And it is connected to other questions. For example, part of the explanation for the adaptation to anti-Semitism that was reflected in the *Militant* coverage of Farrakhan is rooted in elements of lack of clarity on this very question. When a member of the Socialist Workers Party says, as the comrade in Chicago did, that he sees nothing wrong with using the term "white boy," it is not such a big step to the "affectionate" use of terms like "Jew boy." The two terms are not the same, but there is no giant barrier to prevent sliding from one to the other.

This becomes a critical question when we look at it from the standpoint of the construction of a proletarian communist party in this country, which can only be built as a party that reflects in its composition and its leadership at all levels the nationalities and national minorities that make up the working class.

Sometimes young Black or Latino fighters who are new members of the party express attitudes toward comrades who are white that reflect their experiences with racism in this society. These comrades have not yet thought all the way through the need to build a party of the working-class vanguard. They still haven't reached the point of taking the party completely seriously, and seriously seeing themselves as potentially part of the leadership of the proletariat, across all nationalities that make it up.

Like every member has to, these new comrades go through a process in the party, with the help of the party and through experiences, of becoming rounded communists. Comrades who are part of the oppressed nationalities often have not yet crossed the bridge from nationalism to communism before they join. We all need the party for that. Helping them develop as communists is crucial to the development of leadership of the party. But this means working with them, helping them to become Marxists and communist thinkers and fighters. This includes sometimes explaining what's wrong, or incomplete, in some of their thinking.

If we take seriously these comrades developing as leaders of the party, we will take this responsibility seriously. If we were not to accept this responsibility, and act on it, then we would really be saying something else—that we don't think these comrades are capable of assuming responsibility as part of the leadership of the party. If we were to shy away from trying to convince younger comrades of the oppressed nationalities that, for example, race-baiting is totally destructive in the party and an obstacle to the development of communist leadership, we would be saying that we don't really think these comrades have the capacity to be proletarian leaders. We would be, in effect, setting up two kinds of membership in the party—one for comrades of oppressed nationalities who, for whatever reason, we don't believe can become leaders of the working class and of the party; and one for other comrades who can become proletarian leaders. By doing this, of course, we would be placing the biggest obstacle of all in the road of the development of communist leadership throughout the party.

When these points were raised in the discussions in Chicago, substantial progress was achieved. Most comrades had been thinking about this problem, and across the board there was a receptivity to trying to tackle this task in an objective way. As I said before, the fact that comrades in Chicago had been working to find ways to break through the race-baiting that had become a mode of functioning there was what finally forced this matter into the open, and made it possible for the party to deal with it directly, through the elected party bodies and through the Chicago branch.

Following a report to the Political Committee of the results of the Chicago visit I went to the Bay Area. I met with each of the three branch executive committees in the Bay Area, and gave a report to a combined branch meeting of the three branches. I met with each of the National Committee members and with a number of other comrades individually.

At each meeting I asked the same question that I had begun with in Chicago: Is there any evidence of racial prejudice in the functioning of the party in the Bay Area? What emerged was exactly what had emerged in Chicago. There were no examples of racial prejudice but plenty of examples of race-baiting. It had become an established mode of functioning.

In addition to the kinds of examples that had come to light in Chicago, I learned of others. One of the more important of these was an incident that had occurred at the California state convention of the party in the fall of 1983, in the midst of the split of the minority faction. One delegate to the state convention who was a supporter of the majority took the floor and said that the minority faction was composed of racists. By all accounts, no one at that convention—not any of the National Committee members, not the two representatives of the Organization Bureau who were present, not anybody—took the floor to disavow that charge and explain what is wrong with that method of conducting a political debate. Some of the comrades said they had thought it was wrong at the time, but were not sure how to respond to it.

Another example is equally instructive. In the joint branch meeting in the Bay Area, one of the comrades explained that when she had been assigned to the Los Angeles branch she had complained to comrades in the branch leadership that some members of the branch were racists. She said some experienced comrades had responded, "Yes, you are correct but the party is too weak to be able to do anything about it." Many of these comrades who were accused of being racists were later part of the faction that split from the party.

I asked about the basis for the allegation of "racism" of members of the minority faction. No evidence of racism was offered. Instead, political positions of the minority faction members were brought up. For example, the fact that some members of the minority faction had argued against the decision to build fractions in the garment unions was raised to supposedly back up the accusation. Another example offered was the fact that one member of the minority faction had earlier urged a comrade who is Chicano not to change his name from the Anglo one he had grown up with to an Hispanic name. That was the evidence.

What was involved here? First, on the garment fraction perspective. Opposition to building fractions in garment isn't a racist position. It is an expression of opposition to that path of deepening the party's turn to the industrial unions; and it has been in several of the cases mentioned in California part of a disagreement with the political perspective of the turn. But that doesn't make it racist. What's more, raising the accusation of racism doesn't do anything to advance the understanding of the party on the importance of the garment unions for the future of the U.S. working class and the importance to the party today of building fractions in the International Ladies' Garment Workers' Union and the Amalgamated Clothing and Textile Workers Union. It is the kind of "argument" raised when comrades can't explain a political position. It is a substitute for—and therefore an obstacle to—political clarification. It is a crutch. It is an obstacle to dealing with the real problems of building this fraction and comrades feeling free to present their opinions on it.

Isn't that shown by what happened at the 1983 state convention? Instead of helping to clarify the political and organizational issues in dispute with the minority faction a comrade raised the charge of "racism" as a substitute. It did nothing to educate the party, to advance clear thinking and raise the level and freedom of the discussion—just the opposite.

And what about the question of the comrade's Anglo name? Well, maybe the party member who offered this advice thought that the development of some nationalist consciousness that this name-change reflected was not progressive. It could be that the comrade who offered this advice was wrong on the national question in this country, or he didn't understand it, and was opposed to the party's position on it. And even this is speculation. But if so it doesn't make him a racist. Being wrong on the national question didn't make Rosa Luxemburg a racist. It didn't make Trotsky's positions before 1917 on the national question racist positions. They were revolutionaries. And you can be a revolutionary today and not understand the national question, too. And you can be a revolutionary and understand the national question and not change your name.

Making this accusation of racism breeds something else: pressure in the party for comrades to change their names. "Why don't you get rid of your 'slave name'—aren't you a supporter of national pride?" Experience and getting to know the ANC better has helped us on this. We should have learned by now that adopting a Muslim name, or an African name, or an Hispanic name, is not necessarily a sign of whether or not an individual is an uncompromising fighter against national oppression and race discrimination. The opposite can be—and sometimes has been—the case. And of course the difference between a personal and a political decision and the small but important obligation to mind your own business should be remembered.

To call comrades who disagree with the turn or who don't agree with the party's position on nationalism "racists" is race-baiting. It does not advance understanding of the party's position. It reduces the political discussion to name calling. And it is an obstacle to correcting errors and being more concrete on the turn and the place and limits of nationalism—both of which we're doing.

Race-baiting is a refuge of the politically weak and the cliquist; it is a snare and obstacle for the inexperienced. It turns into a crude attempt—regardless of intention—to advance oneself and one's circle. It diminishes party democracy. It is an obstacle to building a leadership that has the respect of the party as a whole.

This is related to another weakness that we have sometimes fallen into: substituting denunciation of something as racist for looking concretely at developments in the class struggle. Rather than trying to place events into the framework of an analysis of actual class forces in conflict, the shifts in relationships between the contending classes, and the need to intervene with the goal of altering that relationship of forces, we sometimes slip into simple-mindedly denouncing some act as "racist." Instead of analyzing—in order to explain—the forms and mechanisms of exploitation, we sometimes fall back on the term "racist" as though it *explains* that exploitation. Instead of examining the working of imperialist oppression—which includes racism, but isn't reducible to it—we can get lazy and be satisfied with condemning an imperialist action as "racist" as though that *explains* it. This lack of clarity can become a real political obstacle. This is especially the case in organizations that are made up entirely of Blacks, or Chicanos, or Puerto Ricans.

Take the National Black Independent Political Party as an example, where being clear on *class politics* is needed for consistent nationalists to move beyond the limits of nationalist positions.

One of the points that I tried to get across to the comrades in the Bay Area and in Chicago is the fact that the cadres of this party take any act of race prejudice in the party seriously—very seriously. The party is more than willing to act decisively to put an immediate end to any manifestations of racial prejudice in this party. We will act regardless of the strength or weakness of a branch. To say that a branch is "too weak" to deal with acts of racial prejudice is, at best, to express complete lack of confidence in the party. This party will not hesitate to act on this—and it would not hesitate to expel comrades if the branch itself won't act on it. Any facts indicating racial prejudice in the party should be brought to the attention of the appropriate leadership body without delay.

However, there is not much fertile ground in this party for racial prejudice. There just isn't. Those who are attracted toward the party are attracted in part by the clarity of the party's stand on this, by its energetic involvement in battles against racial discrimination and oppression, and by the involvement of comrades of oppressed nationalities in all aspects of the party's work and leadership.

But, as our experience has now shown us, race-baiting *can* occur in the party and not be dealt with as quickly as it should be. It is for that reason that race-baiting is a bigger problem than acts of racial prejudice. It was damaging to the party in Chicago. It was an obstacle to the functioning of the elected branch leadership committees. It disrupted the life of the branch—until it was brought into the open and comrades could see what was wrong with it. It gave some comrades who are white the idea that you could fake your way into the leadership by cheerleading for and by being a lawyer for the "needs" of selected comrades of the oppressed nationalities.

The experience of the party, including the discussions in Chicago and the Bay Area, also shows us something else—and something more important. The leadership of the party, including the component of it that is made up of comrades of the oppressed nationalities, is strong enough to deal with this problem. The party leadership includes a significant layer of comrades of the oppressed nationalities. This is true in the National Committee, it is true in the Political Committee and the leadership committees directly responsible to it, and it is true at the branch level. And it is especially true for comrades who are Black.

This is no small accomplishment. What this party has accomplished on this front has never been done before in this country. There has never been a revolutionary communist party in this country with a leadership that cuts across racial lines as much as the SWP leadership does today. In fact, it is our judgment that the SWP is among those parties that have made the greatest progress toward the goal of a genuinely nonracial leadership (in the sense the African National Congress uses the term) of a revolutionary party in the imperialist countries. We haven't finished the process—but we've taken big strides in this direction over the last decade and a half.

And that is why we can have this discussion and settle this problem by eliminating this obstacle to the development of communist leadership. Questions like this one tend to get posed in front of the party as a whole only when they are capable of being solved—not before.

A similar thing happened a decade ago when the question of Black and "Third World" exclusive social affairs got posed, and resolved, by the party as a whole, at the 1977 convention. (See "Leninist Norms and Nonexclusive Party Social Affairs," by Catarino Garza, reprinted in this bulletin.)

These so-called "social affairs" began to take on the tone and content of a Black caucus and became an obstacle to the development of leaders of the party who are Black. Those exclusive "social affairs" finally came to an end when enough of the comrades who are Black or Chicano or Puerto Rican had reached the point of seeing themselves as leaders of the party, not just as leaders of other comrades who are Black. Enough of us had gotten to the point where we were ready to take responsibility for leading the party. Therefore, we no longer felt we had to lean on the crutch of "social affairs" that were really also political meetings along racial lines.

A tendency toward caucuses of comrades of the oppressed nationalities is almost always present to some degree because of the nature of this racist society. It gets expressed inside the party as a result of the pressures being exerted on the party.

One of the most negative sides of the mode of functioning that drifts toward some kind of "Black caucus" is a simultaneous push away from the comrades who are Black taking more and more responsibility for the leadership of the party as a whole. It tends to begin breeding and reinforcing an attitude of competition between comrades who are Black. It becomes an arena where a two-bit contest—sometimes hidden, sometimes open— over pecking order among the "brothers" and "sisters" rears its head. We would see a situation where development of leadership of Blacks in the party would be seen as occurring in competition with other comrades who are Black. Comrades of the oppressed nationalities who don't go along are themselves badmouthed. We would get concerns over the "pecking order" among comrades who are Black. After all, you would only need so many "Black leaders" to lead the "Black members." Too many leaders would then be a problem. What an obstacle this would be!

Similar points could be made regarding comrades who are Chicano or Puerto Rican or from other oppressed nationalities.

Now we are in a position to resolve this question of race-baiting. If we were to back away from acting decisively on it, it would set us back. If we didn't act, we would be saying in reality that we are going to have a communist party not of equals, but of unequals. We would be saying that some members are going to be allowed to follow different rules, different norms. We would be saying that comrades who are Black or Latino aren't going to be held responsible for functioning under the same standards of membership and leadership as others. We would be saying that there are some comrades who just can't be expected to be communists. They are incapable of leading all sections of the party, all sections of the working class, of having the *same undifferentiated and objective* relationship to *all* members of the party. The standard of personal and political conduct toward the party they will be held to has to be modified, downward, to their level. This is the opposite of the experience of the party the last 15 years.

This would be throwing obstacles in the road of the development of communist leaders who are Black, Puerto Rican, and Chicano. This would lead the party in the opposite direction from what we have been conquering in the last decade-and-a-half. This would cripple our proletarian orientation and internationalist foundations.

The policy we are adopting today is both possible and necessary to implement. Race-baiting is an obstacle to proletarian norms of functioning, and a barrier to the development of party leadership. It is incompatible with membership in the party.

CHILDREN, CHILD CARE, AND MEMBERSHIP NORMS OF A PROLETARIAN PARTY
Report adopted by SWP Political Committee, June 18, 1986

by Jack Barnes

All members of the Political Committee have received three items: the letter from James; the letter from Vivian; and the motions from the executive committee and from James and Cris that were discussed at the June 1 St. Louis branch meeting.

The issues that have come up for debate in the St. Louis branch point to the need to review our policies with regard to three matters: 1) the problems of child care for party members who have children; 2) the presence of children at party meetings; and 3) the question raised by Cris concerning breast feeding by party members at political meetings or gatherings, including internal party meetings.

The discussion in the St. Louis branch has centered on the third question, but this cannot be dealt with adequately without addressing the other two.

Character of the party

Two counterposed approaches toward deciding these policies emerge from the descriptions of the discussion in the St. Louis branch provided by the letters from James and Vivian. One approach starts from the standpoint of the party, and how the party can best organize to help create the conditions for each and every member to have a productive political life and to do their best to build the revolutionary movement. The other approach strays from politics onto theories about breast feeding, "parenting," and the "rights of mothers." This approach starts looking for how the party can adjust its functioning to bring it in line with these considerations.

Our starting point is the kind of party that we are and that we are trying to build. This is summarized in the initial report on the turn to the industrial unions adopted in 1978, as well as in the various reports on party leadership adopted by the party since that time.

[See "Leading the Party into Industry," the report adopted by the February 1978 National Committee meeting, in *The Changing Face of U.S. Politics*, pp. 154–98 [2011 printing]; the National Committee reports on party leadership by Jack Barnes and Mary-Alice Waters that are collected in the June 1985 *Information Bulletin* on preparing the election of the National Committee (No. 2 in 1985); and "Revolutionary Perspective and Leninist Continuity in the United States," 1984–85 political resolution of the Socialist Workers Party, especially Part IV, "The Turn to the Industrial Unions and the Party's Political Continuity," in *New International*, No. 4, Spring 1985.]

The character of the party and of its norms is an especially important question for us now, because of the modest but real recruitment opportunities for the Young Socialist Alliance and the Socialist Workers Party. New members will be educated in, adjust to, and adopt the norms of the movement they join. If there is a gap between what we *say* and what we *do*, new members will—correctly—emulate our deeds more than our words.

We are building a party that strives to be proletarian in composition as well as in program. We're building a *political* party, an organization of cadres that is *part* of the working class, a political fraction of our class. As the 1978 report on the turn put it, we are building a party of worker-Bolsheviks.

"A worker-Bolshevik," the report explained, "is someone who at all times takes on major responsibility as part of a party team, in whatever way it is necessary. A worker-Bolshevik is a comrade who is ready at any time to be full-time at the request of the party, who sustains financially and supports politically the professional full-time staff of the apparatus, the press, the machinery the party needs to function."

We're building a party of politically active workers who function in the class struggle on the basis of collective experiences, with a democratically arrived-at line, with a common mode of activity and with a shared commitment. Those who *do,* decide. And those who *decide,* implement.

We take a class approach to recruitment to the party. We seek above all to recruit workers. We seek to win fighters to our ranks—those who we are fighting alongside in the unions; in the struggle for Black rights; in the campaigns against U.S. intervention in Central America and against support to the apartheid regime; in the fight for women's rights; and so on. We pay special attention to the recruitment of workers of the oppressed nationalities; of women workers; and of youth—on the job, out of the high schools, and off the college campuses.

We aim to win to the party individuals who can develop the political, mental, and physical discipline to become committed proletarian revolutionists.

We are building a party of the working class, and the working class in capitalist society is not homogeneous. It is a differentiated class—differentiated between employed and unemployed, between urban and rural, by job and job classification, by national origin and nationality, by sex, by age, by political experience, between those with children and those with no children, and in numerous other ways. These differentiations—those purely social in origin imposed by the rulers, those with a biological dimension, and those rooted in a combination of the two—are used by the exploiting classes to keep the workers and our allies divided, in order to expand profits and maintain capitalist rule. More important, the social use of these differentiations by the employers and government is reinforced and reproduced by the workings of the capitalist market economy itself.

A working-class party will also attract individuals from other classes to its ranks, above all from among working farmers and other toiling producers and from some layers of the middle class. This will bring other differentiations in background into its ranks.

From the widely differentiated individuals that join it, the party's job is to forge a cadre that is programmatically undifferentiated. Its job is to recruit from socially heterogeneous working people in order, through common experience and education, to build a politically homogeneous working-class party.

We can't and don't try to equalize inside the party the differentiated conditions of various individuals who join. For example, we don't require that members turn over personal property and income to the party. We are a workers' party, financed first and foremost by the voluntary contributions of the membership. We're not a utopian commune or society of levelers.

But the party rejects accepting any of these differences as the basis for *political* differentiations among comrades. We are all SWPers, under the same party constitution, with the same rights and requirements of membership, and entitled to the party's best efforts to make possible a rewarding political life.

The capitalists turn a blind eye to the demonstrated capacities and abilities of workers, Blacks and other oppressed national minorities, and women. The rulers promote and play on every form of prejudice, bigotry, and discrimination.

The communist movement does the opposite. We look for and encourage the development of political abilities of working-class comrades—being specially alert to those who are Black or from other oppressed national minorities and to those who are women. The party offers all of its members the same opportunities to function as political equals in the class struggle, to develop as leaders of the party and leaders of the working class.

Vivian put this very well in her letter, reflecting on her own experience as a woman who joined the SWP at a time in her life when she had already had three children. ". . . one of the things I most appreciated about the party when I first came around it," Vivian wrote, "was that in contrast to the rest of the world that was telling me all the things I couldn't do because now I had to be a responsible parent, the party opened doors to me the same way it did to every other comrade and put no limits on my participation."

Organizing a party of workers

Since the turn to the industrial unions eight years ago, we have taken many steps to promote the fullest participation by workers in the party's political activity. Many branches have changed the day and time of weekly membership meetings and executive committee meetings. We have learned to organize agendas to avoid going on late into the night. Sometimes we have to organize two meetings to account for workers on different shifts. The changing class composition of the party and our milieus has altered our criteria in the scheduling of forums and classes, committee meetings, and meetings of the industrial union fractions.

The party also seeks to help comrades who have children to organize ways to solve the problem of child care in order to maximize their participation in political life. This problem wouldn't come up if we were an organization oriented to middle-class professionals, who possess the financial resources to afford professional child care. But we're not. We're a party of working people.

Responsibility for child care rests with the individual members who have children, not with the party or any other members of the party. The party cannot and does not try to compensate for the lack of adequate, government-funded child-care facilities (or medical care or other necessary social services). But that doesn't settle the question at all.

The party, for example, pays attention to the organization of child care at national conferences. The committee in charge of conference arrangements helps organize a service so that comrades with children can participate in all the political activities during the week. This is accomplished through a combination of professional facilities, paid for by the parents who use them, and supplementary child care organized and staffed by those conference participants who have brought children with them.

We think that we can have the best child-care program ever at this year's conference. If we succeed, it will be largely due to the initiative of two comrades who are parents and our response to their suggestions.

Toward the end of last year's conference, two party members from Phoenix who are parents—Bernie and Sue—raised a number of problems they had noted with the organization of child care at the gathering, as well as some ideas for improvements. To follow up on that discussion, the Organization Bureau has arranged for Bernie to fly into New York for a day or two this summer to participate in planning the organization of child care at the upcoming August national conference. Bernie has volunteered to work with the Organization Bureau and the conference arrangements committee prior to and during the conference to help organize and coordinate the child care.

The question of child care for party members with children was taken up in the women's liberation resolution adopted by the 1979 World Congress of the Fourth International. That resolution was also adopted by a big majority at the August 1979 SWP convention.

". . . the leadership has the obligation to work with comrades who have family responsibilities to try to find collective solutions that will enable them to minimize the obstacles to their political activity. . . .

"At the same time, we recognize that there are limits to what the party can do. The party itself cannot assume the material obligation to eliminate the economic and social inequalities among comrades created by class society. We cannot assure the social services capitalism does not provide. The party does not have a generalized obligation to provide child care in order to equalize the personal situations of all comrades, nor can child-care duties be imposed on any comrade."

Political pressures

Each of us comes into the party from a particular background and with a particular personal situation. And each of us has to make all sorts of individual decisions that to a greater or lesser degree have consequences for our political activity in the party. The job of the party in this regard is not to issue orders or to lay down guidelines on matters that cannot be the party's responsibility or business. Rather, the party's job is to educate, encourage, and inspire comrades to become the kind of serious revolutionists who, over the long haul, make those choices that enable them to function politically as committed, responsible cadres and leaders of the party and of the working-class movement.

Over the past half decade or so, the pressures from the capitalist economic and political offensive have come down with increasing intensity on the working class in this country. The leadership report by Mary-Alice Waters adopted by the

May 1985 National Committee meeting explained that these pressures weigh especially heavily on women in capitalist society.

"Women who are full-time industrial workers and part of the union movement are in the best position to resist the conservatizing pressures that all women are subjected to by this economic and political offensive of the ruling class," the report explained. "These women—among whom are most of the women who are members of our movement—have a greater degree of confidence that comes from knowing that they can sell their labor power and survive, thus being able to have some small element of independence in making important decisions affecting their lives. They have acquired at least the beginning of class consciousness through understanding that they have a better chance of improving wages and working conditions by joining together with fellow workers to fight the employer. Moreover, despite the bosses' attempts to foster animosity, women in industry are frequently working alongside male co-workers in job situations where each depends on the other and relations of mutual confidence can develop."

The report pointed out that women who are communists are also more politically conscious and have the advantage of being part of an organized workers' party. These facts, however, do not mean that comrades—female or male—in the party and in the party's industrial union fractions escape the pressures.

"We're part of our class," the report continued, "and the offensive on women's rights is aimed at our class above all." Women comrades who are in industry "are constantly fighting the suggestions that we're not really workers; that it is a temporary condition; that the important thing is that we are women; that women are only a marginal part of the working class; that we are not hereditary proletarians; that we work for a while and then we leave the work force to raise a family; that we work part time or on and off, switching jobs. We're constantly being told that what really defines our lives is not selling our labor power, but home and husband and children.

"Because we work with men and women who are generally more influenced than we by the attitudes and assumptions fostered by the rulers' pervasive propaganda, the truth is that we find it harder today than we did five years ago to simply be ourselves with our coworkers. It's harder to simply be the kind of women (and men) we are: women who are class conscious, political, workers. Communists. Women whose being is not defined by children and family. Women whose interests are focused on being active builders of the revolutionary workers' movement, from which we derive great satisfaction. That's who we are."

The political retreat of the working class in the face of the capitalist offensive has also slowed the pace of recruitment to the party over the past decade and led to a substantial net loss in membership. The average age of comrades has gone up, and this too has magnified the pressures on party members—if anything, more so on women. "It is a simple fact of life in class society that aging takes a bigger toll on women than on men," the National Committee report explained.

"Women are taught by all their life experiences, by all the ways they are molded and conditioned in this society, that it is all over by the time you hit 40. You're over the hill. You're no longer of any interest to men. And if you've got a man, you better hold onto him, because you won't get another one.

"You're too old to reproduce, so you have no use value any more. That's another theme we've seen in article after article over the last few years—the dangers of having children too late in life. They are aimed at women in their 20s and 30s, and the message is clear. You better have that kid now. If you don't, you'll be sorry, because the likelihood is that any child you give birth to a few years from now will be retarded or deformed. And it will be your fault, because you selfishly wanted to postpone having children until you were too old to produce a healthy baby."

These considerations help explain both the sharp increase in this country in childbearing among women in their 30s, and are also a factor in the rise in teenage pregnancy rates.

These kinds of pressures are always at work in capitalist society, the report explained, "but they are exacerbated by the slow advance of the working-class movement and the slow pace of recruitment today. Women aren't carried along by a rising movement. The difficulties seem greater, the solutions fewer, the struggle more protracted."

In thinking about the political questions that

underlie the dispute in the St. Louis branch, it is useful to go back and review that May 1985 National Committee report. These questions are also addressed in the new Pathfinder book, *Cosmetics, Fashions, and the Exploitation of Women,* most directly in the introduction based on the report adopted by the National Committee.

The 'personal' and the 'political': a false dichotomy

James reports that some members in St. Louis were concerned that the discussion in the branch was "an intrusion into a comrade's personal affairs." James disagreed with this view. Whether or not to breast feed a child is clearly not a question of party concern. But the decision to do so at political meetings or gatherings, including internal party meetings, has direct political consequences. So does the question of having children present at party meetings. These are not decisions that should be left to the parents. These are political matters for collective decision by the party.

We should avoid the false dichotomy between the "personal" and the "political."

First, the word "personal," or "private," is often used when the word "individual" is really more correct. Every choice we make is an individual decision, whether on a political question related to the party and the class struggle, or on a matter concerning our personal or private lives and relationships. Often, what we are really trying to distinguish are individual decisions from collective decisions, or decisions that have substantial political consequences from those that do not.

In addition to the individual decisions that are directly political, all party members also make many other decisions that do not have direct political consequences for the party or the working-class movement as a whole. The party has no position on most of them. It tries to stay out of comrades' personal business. Workers don't like nosy parties any more than nosy neighbors.

Some personal choices, of course, do have political consequences for individual members, sometimes big ones. A comrade may make a personal decision to live in a particular city, irrespective of party considerations. Other personal decisions can affect the amount of time a member devotes to political responsibilities; the type of job and income level a member considers acceptable; the size of one's sustainer and other voluntary financial contributions to the party; one's willingness to take a full-time assignment; and so on.

Each individual member has to weigh these political consequences as he or she makes such personal decisions. The decisions that we make vary at different points in our lives. Sometimes things are more difficult; we all do better at some times than at others. The party cannot and does not intervene in such decisions or have a policy on them. It does not hold these decisions against any comrade.

Instead, the party establishes norms of activity and discipline expected of the entire membership and encourages each and every member—in an undifferentiated way—to take on as much political responsibility and leadership as he or she is able and willing to do.

Certain individual choices can have political consequences that make these decisions the business of the party for collective discussion and action. The party does not meddle, "officially" or not, in the emotional relationships of its members, for example. But this does not mean that the party takes no position on whether or not a male member beats his female companion or wife. We enforce a policy against violence by party members against women inside or outside the party, as part of our general policy against violence inside the party and the workers' movement.

The party has no policy on who comrades date. But if a member starts going out with a cop, a foreman, or a virulent racist in the plant, then this becomes a political matter for action by the party.

We have no policy on what comrades do to relax. But we do have a policy against the use by party members of illegal drugs and comrades' presence at social gatherings or on premises where they know or have good reason to believe that such drugs are being used or kept.

There is no inseparable line between what are commonly called "personal" or "private" or "emotional" matters, on the one hand, and "political" or "party" or "public" matters, on the other. On some questions such as violence and illegal drugs, the party has clearly spelled-out policies, but there is not and cannot be some exhaustive list of "do's" and "don't's."

As professional revolutionists, party members subordinate personal considerations to political considerations when the two come into conflict. Those individuals who place top priority on personal or private matters—be it friends, family, a job, a hobby, or whatever—don't join the party and don't commit their lives to building the revolutionary workers' movement.

All these questions have become even more important for the party since our turn to the industrial unions. Politically serious coworkers who collaborate with and get to know the party watch how we act, how we treat each other, how we treat other workers and people that we work with. And when we recruit coworkers to the party, they will tend to emulate the norms and standards that they see in practice in our movement.

Keeping in mind these considerations about the character of the party and party norms, let's take a look at the particular issues posed by the dispute in the St. Louis branch.

Why children should not be present at party meetings

The first substantial question of party policy is posed by the fact that a child was present at the St. Louis branch membership meeting.

The SWP has a longstanding policy against having children present at branch meetings and other party political meetings and classes. This was reaffirmed in a report adopted by the National Committee in April 1971. [See the excerpt from this 1971 report printed as an appendix.]

The reason for this policy is simple. The presence of children at branch meetings leads to noise and other distractions that interfere with the conduct of the business of the branch. The same holds true for meetings of branch committees and fractions.

(This is quite different from, say, a branch picnic, where we encourage comrades and coworkers to bring their friends and families, including children.)

The branch meeting provides a weekly opportunity for all members to participate, on an equal basis, in common, collective discussion and decision-making on how best to carry out the party's tasks and campaigns in their area. This requires that all those attending the meeting be in the same position to hear the reports and discussion, to ask for the floor, to vote when the time comes, and to take part in an educational—without unnecessary distractions, without having to come in and out of the meeting hall for stints on child care in another room, and so on.

This becomes impossible if children are present at the meeting, or if the branch gets into the child-care business in a room adjoining the meeting hall. Aside from the problems already mentioned, the members who have children can't participate fully in the meeting, and pressures build to adjust branch business around the child care. The members who are parents have to divide their attention between the meeting and the children—missing part of a report or discussion, being out of the room when they might like to speak, missing a vote, and so on. Or else the branch starts altering its agenda—putting off a report and discussion until later in the meeting so that someone involved in the work can come back in the room, postponing a vote because a member is on a child-care stint (and has thus missed all or part of the discussion), and so on. All this gets in the way of the democracy of the branch decision-making process, the only process that can lead to a *politically* homogenous party.

For comrades who are parents, participation in the branch meeting requires being freed up from other responsibilities for a couple of hours to concentrate their attention on politics, just like other members of the branch organize to free themselves from other obligations to attend the meeting. The same considerations hold for other political meetings at the headquarters.

As previously explained, the party should work with comrades who have children to help them solve the particular problem of organizing for child care, so that they can participate fully in all party meetings and other political activities they are able to attend. This is easier at national conferences than on a branch level, because of the limited duration of such gatherings and the greater ease in organizing professional assistance during the major sessions.

Handling this in a branch may involve the parents pooling resources to hire baby-sitters, or taking other individual or collective steps to fit a given situation. This may even mean that one or another member has to miss a meeting or activity occasionally, just as comrades do for various other personal or job-related reasons off and on. This is preferable to a situation that institutionalizes distractions from branch business for members who have children and don't have children alike.

One further point. Although the party has no expertise or positions on child-rearing, I remain convinced that being dragged to branch meetings and other party political gatherings is not good for the children themselves. They get bored and restless. A lot of participants trying to concentrate on the meeting, class, or forum either ignore the children, glare at them, or shush them. It's not a good atmosphere for kids.

'Rights of mothers'
It is important to be clear on the political basis for the party's approach to its collaboration with comrades to help them find workable solutions to the problems of child care. This is not a matter of "special rights" of parents who are members of the SWP. James is correct in his letter on the dispute in the St. Louis branch that, "One group approached the question from the role of the revolutionary party and its cadres in the class and how we present ourselves, and the other from the rights of mothers in the party and how they personally felt about it."

There are no special "rights of mothers" in the SWP.

There is also no basis for the view—described by James in his letter—that the party "wishes to push mothers out or more correctly can't assimilate women with children." Just the opposite. No assignment or leadership task in the party is out of bounds to any comrade because of her or his personal situation. The SWP is one of the few organizations in U.S. society in which a woman who has children is treated not as a mother or female, but as a worker, as an equal, as a political human being, as a potential leader of the working class.

Each member is approached objectively and politically, on the basis of what she or he can do to help build the revolutionary movement.

Different norms for internal and public activity?
Another important question that should be clarified is the one raised by the straw poll taken in the St. Louis branch on the question, to quote James's letter, of "whether comrades thought that the decision against breast feeding should not be enforced in a branch meeting but should be prohibited in our public political work. . . ." Toward the end of the letter, James explains his own view on this question:

"I reject and find dangerous the concept that comrades should be able to function differently in branch meetings than we would in other meetings of our class. I think ideas like this can only tend toward our isolation from the class and make us less confident about recruitment, doing work in the unions and the class as a whole. It also tends in the direction of viewing branch meetings as gatherings of friends in a somewhat larger living room, rather than a serious political meeting."

Vivian also comments on this aspect of the branch discussion in her letter:

"My question is why we would want to do things in branch meetings that we wouldn't be comfortable with in union meetings? How can we fit this idea with the idea that we want to recruit new people to our party? Will we be more confident in asking people to join our party if it means that we'll be asking them to come to meetings where we have different norms of conduct? Do we have a 'public' face and a 'private' one? Are we, who are already in the party, some advanced breed, or are we a political party made up of people who work together based on a particular set of political ideas and goals?"

These are very important questions for the party.

There is no acceptable difference for members of the SWP in their norms of conduct inside and outside the party. Contrary to those who red-bait the communist movement, we have no dual or hidden agendas. Just as we don't *say* one thing internally and another in unions and in the mass movement, we don't *act* one way internally and another way in public.

To operate on any other basis will not equip us to go out of branch meetings and present our views in an effective way to other working people. If we cannot explain a political question clearly and objectively in a branch meeting, then we will not be able to do so when we explain it in a union meeting, an antiwar coalition, or elsewhere. If we rely in the branch on lingo, jargon, and in-group assumptions, then we will fail both in educating and politicizing our own members and in arming them to convince other working people of our views.

The same holds true of how we conduct ourselves inside and outside the party. If our weekly membership meetings are not well-organized political gatherings, designed to make decisions on how the branch carries out its work, then that lack of seriousness and professionalism will spill over into every aspect of our public work. The way we organize ourselves, our headquarters, and our internal and public gatherings will affect how we function in the unions and elsewhere in the mass movement. Our ability to treat each other in an objective and comradely way inside the party will increase our capacity to collaborate with coworkers, contacts, and others in all aspects of our political work.

These problems of turning inward increase in the party during a political retreat. We tend to fall into the use of jargon, since we spend more and more time talking to each other, as opposed to workers not in the SWP. There are pressures toward clique and "family" modes of functioning. Understanding why such tendencies are corrosive to the party is the beginning of wisdom in counteracting them, and our efforts to do so will be both easier and even more important as we turn the party outward toward new recruitment opportunities.

Vivian is correct in rejecting the notion that the distinguishing characteristic of membership in a revolutionary workers' party is that we are some "advanced breed" of human beings. The revolutionary party is the political vanguard of the working class, not the cell of the new society. There are kinds of behavior that are incompatible with party membership: violence, racist or anti-woman language or actions, scabbing, and others. But these are things that we actively fight against within the workers' movement as a whole, not just standards of conduct inside the SWP.

There are, of course, certain organizational norms in the party that differ from those that we may advocate at any particular time in the unions or in the mass movement. We do not advocate women's caucuses or Black caucuses in the SWP, for example, while we sometimes do support a struggle for such formations in a union situation. But this is because the bureaucratization of the unions often makes it necessary for specially oppressed layers of the working class to organize along such lines in order to advance an uncompromising struggle for their rights and the rights of the ranks as a whole against the capitalists and for equality within the labor movement. If problems along these lines exist in a party that claims to be revolutionary, we might well support the formation of caucuses in such an organization.

'Public opinion'

Should the SWP have a policy that members not publicly breast feed a child at political gatherings on the grounds that, as the letter from James puts it, "public breast feeding [is] not a cultural norm in our country," or isn't "an accepted practice in North American culture"?

No. Public opinion in capitalist society is always *bourgeois* public opinion. We don't adopt bourgeois public opinion as a guideline for norms of party membership.

What concerns the SWP is not the norm in "our" country, or in "North American culture." We are concerned about what is normal and comfortable among workers in this country today. Class-struggle-minded workers that we collaborate with in the labor movement will expect SWP members to conduct themselves so as not to create unnecessary problems for our joint work.

What we have to offer to the rest of the working class is a political perspective that clarifies our common historic line of march. We do not want to erect any unnecessary obstacles to our participation alongside other working people in the battles that can change society, and to recruitment of more workers to the revolutionary party.

Whether in a branch meeting, at a union meeting, at a rally to demand the arrest of killer cops, or at any other political gathering, publicly nursing a baby is not currently the norm in the working class in this country. Exceptions are just that—exceptions. Breast feeding in public gatherings attracts attention and makes many people—both those already in our movement, and those whom we want to win to our movement—uncomfortable. That is simply a fact. Maybe it won't be someday. It is today.

The problem is not how a woman who is a member of the party and who has a baby chooses to feed her child. That is her right and her responsibility. This is not a moral question. The party has no moral objection whatsoever to breast feeding. But the party, unlike bourgeois public opinion, also ascribes no negative moral content to many other natural biological acts that are nonetheless unacceptable at internal or public political gatherings.

Vivian points out that some of those in the St. Louis branch who opposed the executive committee proposal argued that comrades "can get used to it or just not look." Vivian correctly rejects this argument.

James is also correct in his letter to reject "the idea that those who were against breast feeding in the branch were backward and that those who ignored it or better yet weren't conscious of it were more progressive-thinking; as though being unconscious of something is morally superior to being aware of it."

People *do* notice, and many are made uncomfortable. No member, friend, or contact of the party should feel under pressure to "get used to it or just not look." That is petty bourgeois utopianism, not communism. This has nothing to do with some alleged lack of political "progressive-mindedness." What unites members of a revolutionary workers' party is not that we are some especially "progressive-thinking" sector of society, but that we are a political selection of our class bound together by commitment to a common program and by collective class-struggle experience.

Why, at a political meeting, should party members have to "get used to not looking" at something that a member of the party is doing in the room? That kind of atmosphere cannot possibly be conducive to a serious, democratic decision-making meeting.

Nor can a branch meeting be a gathering of political equals if some members are occupied in breast feeding a child, while others are occupied in trying "not to notice." The member who is breast feeding cannot participate on an equal basis in the political discussion, so she will inevitably begin not to be treated as an equal by other members.

James and Vivian explain that Cris, in motivating her countermotion to that of the executive committee, pointed to the acquittal of a woman in a St. Louis court who had been charged with indecent exposure for breast feeding her baby in her car. If the facts are correct, then this court decision was a step forward for women's rights.

But what does this have to do with determining party policy? Our policy is not based on any idea that breast feeding in public is or may be illegal. Our policy has to do with conducting ourselves in our political work in such a way as to create no unnecessary barriers to winning and integrating workers into our movement.

Is breast feeding 'scientifically progressive'?

James explains that, "Cris's counterreport [to the June 1 branch meeting] basically explained the benefits of breast feeding and suggested that comrades should learn more about it." Another comrade, Vivian adds, "said that there was a 'new trend' in breast feeding in the women's movement . . . that the branch should catch up on." According to Vivian, Cris "urged the branch to read various books on this question to get educated on it."

The party does not establish its norms on the basis of what may be currently considered "progressive trends" in science or the arts by some sectors of bourgeois public opinion, or by various currents in other social movements. The attempt to have the party take a position on such "progressive" scientific or cultural questions actually fetishizes science and the arts, confusing them with fads.

Middle-class reformers often peddle "scientific" nostrums that are actually anti-working-class in content. They rationalize regressive cigarette and beer taxes, for example, by pointing to the "health benefits," thereby adding to the tax load on working people while the lives of the wealthy are unaffected.

Today many doctors, books on child-rearing, and the media explain all sorts of things that "all good mothers" must do if they don't want to ruin their children's lives—most of which are beyond the time and resources of working-class women. "Specialists" wag their fingers at women workers for "selfishly" spending too little time at home with their young children.

An example of this is one of the books that Cris urged comrades to read to learn more about breast feeding, according to Vivian's letter. The book, entitled *The Womanly Art of Breastfeeding*, is put out by a group called La Leche League. It may or may not include some medical information that could be of use to a breast feeding mother; I'm not qualified to judge. But its political message is plainly reactionary.

First, the book urges that a mother spend at least the first three years after birth at home with her child. It approvingly quotes the ominous warning by one doctor that, "Too much disruption of this embeds in the personality [of the child] traits that can be destructive for a lifetime."

Second, the book glorifies women who have decided to give up their jobs altogether in order to be "a full-time mother." If this is impossible for financial reasons, the author advises, "Many kinds of office work can be done just as well at home, so you might be able to interest your employer in having you do part-time work at home, coming into the office just long enough to pick up and deliver your work." Thus, the book endorses the accelerating drive by the capitalists to weaken the unions, drive down wages, and gut regulated working conditions by institutionalizing homework, part-time work, and Manpower or Kelly Girl–style temporary jobs for growing layers of the working class, female and male.

Third, the book adds fuel to the propaganda campaign to justify more cutbacks in government-funded child-care facilities. "Group care in a day-care center," it claims, "falls far short of meeting a baby's or toddler's need to relate to one person, to count on one person for loving attention all of the time, at any time. Basically, little ones are homebodies." And their mothers should be too—that's the message.

All this is what Vivian refers to in her letter as the "'be there for your child' package." She adds: "I don't know if more working-class women are breast feeding today. It's certainly not a new invention. I do doubt if many working-class women have the option of breast feeding for years at a time. Perhaps it is only something else for us working mothers to feel guilty about."

The party has no position on breast feeding, pro or con, and should not. It does, however, reject telling working-class women who choose to bottle feed their children, for whatever reason, that they are doing something wrong. That they should be breast feeding their babies instead. That they are harming their children. This is simply another example of anti-working-class prejudice being falsely touted as "science."

The party does reject telling women that they should stay home, give up their jobs, or settle for low wages and no union protection by doing homework or taking a part-time or temporary job. Or that child care will ruin their children's future.

To the contrary. Women workers, with or without children, need to be in the vanguard of those pressing the labor movement to combat the attacks by the employing class on union rights, job conditions, prolabor legislation, and social services.

James makes a number of good points on this in his letter. "There is also a great deal of 'claptrap' passed off as science on the best way of raising children, . . ." he writes. "There is a tendency to place the dynamics of the class struggle in second place to good parenting techniques.

"I bring this up," James continues, "because this became part of our discussion on breast feeding, as to why it was superior to bottle feeding. At this point, the party has no position on this; I don't think it should. . . .

"I personally think discussions about raising the perfect or near-perfect child have a reactionary tinge to them that places nurturing above the class struggle, and tends in the direction of defining women comrades as mothers or nurturers rather than as comrades."

Our goal is to recruit and educate workers, women and men, who are attracted to the SWP on the basis of our political positions and our activity in the unions and the mass movement—not on the basis of this or that view about breast feeding, jogging, a high-fiber diet, music, sports, or so on. It's fine for comrades to pursue their own personal views and inclinations on such matters, but they are not the business of the party.

Vivian's letter, after pointing to some of these important considerations, adds: "Sometimes breast feeding is a political issue. We ran articles . . . when women in underdeveloped countries led a campaign against the Nestlé's corporation because they did not have access to clean drinking water for baby formula—something the profit-hungry company didn't care a thing about. (This example was raised by a comrade in the branch to show that breast feeding is progressive.)"

But breast feeding was not the issue in the campaign to expose Nestlé. The question was the greed of a major imperialist-owned corporation that foisted an unhealthy product onto children in Asia, Africa, and Latin America in order to boost its profits, regardless of the cost in human life and misery. We and other revolutionists had no trouble taking a clear stand on this political issue of imperialist exploitation and racist murder without taking a position on breast feeding vs. bottle feeding.

Recruitment of women

The letter from James explains that Cris, in her counterreport, expressed the view that a policy against breast feeding at party meetings "would push women away from being able to fully participate in our politics." James reports that during the branch discussion another comrade said that such a policy "would prevent us from recruiting women."

Is this true? Are we making it more difficult to recruit women, above all women workers, to the SWP? Are we making it more difficult for women to develop into leaders of the party and of the working class?

No. To the contrary. The SWP will continue to recruit women, including women who have children. But we will recruit them to communism and to a communist party—just as we do all those who join. They don't enter our ranks with a second-class ticket. We approach them as part of our class, as fighters from the working class, not as women, not as mothers, not as homemakers who also happen to hold down a job—not as they are treated by virtually every other organization and institution in capitalist society.

The party's turn to industry is the bedrock of our ability to continue to help women members advance politically. As the May 1985 National Committee report by Mary-Alice Waters explained:

"We aren't *more* susceptible to the ideological counteroffensive of the ruling class because we are more working-class in social composition and milieu. Just the opposite. . . . If our membership and milieu were primarily middle-class, middle-aged radical and ex-radical professionals and white collar workers, we know what kind of conservative, despairing conclusions we would be adapting to."

A graphic illustration is provided by the front-page feature article in the March–April 1986 issue of *Democratic Left,* published by the Democratic Socialists of America (DSA).

Headlined "Sandbox Socialism: Can We Pass the Torch?", this article draws the opposite conclusion on every important question of politics and organization that has been dealt with in this report. Author Maxine Phillips opens the article with the following paragraph:

"Will DSA lose not just one but two generations of activists to the new 'baby boom?' It's no news that the generation in the 30 to 40-year-old age range is having babies and becoming less active in DSA, but when *Democratic Left* surveyed both new and experienced parents to find out what the organization could do to help them stay active, it found that parents are looking for more than child care during meetings. They want their children to become involved. The news is that if DSA doesn't appeal to parents *and* children, it risks losing both generations."

The article advocates a number of solutions. The organization itself should provide child care for parents at all DSA internal or public events; it approvingly raises the idea that members with no children should be given the full responsibility for rotating half-hour stints. In fact, DSA events should increasingly be organized around the special needs of children, and of those parents in the organization who are retreating from politics.

Finally, the article suggests that a "Parenting Caucus" might be a good idea for the DSA. Such a caucus, it says, could have a positive political impact on the organization. "Parents' groups are often highly motivated on certain issues. When asked if having children had changed their political interests, DSA parents cited education, day care, sex-role stereotyping, racism, the environment, and especially nuclear war, as taking on more importance."

The SWP does not need a "Parenting Caucus" to deepen the determination of our members, female and male, to build a proletarian-led mass revolutionary movement to rid the United States and the world of these and other economic, social, and political ills of the imperialist system. That task requires the construction of a vanguard internationalist party that is proletarian in its program, in its organizational norms, and in the composition of its membership and leadership. A communist party. That's the kind of party that we have set out to build.

The capitalists and their propagandists want women to see themselves as women, not as workers, not as fighters and leaders from the working class. The employers' aim is to depress the value of the labor power of women workers and thereby drive down the value of labor power for the working class as a whole. Our aim, on the other hand, is to help women become cadres and leaders of the revolutionary working-class movement that will overthrow the system that is responsible for their special oppression as women and for their superexploitation as workers.

That is what the revolutionary party holds out to women. The opportunity to become a leader of the working class and of the revolutionary party. The opportunity to become part of the fight to build a powerful movement for women's rights, and to bring the power of the unions into the center of that battle. The opportunity to become a leader in the fight against imperialist war, against racism, against environmental destruction. The opportunity to be treated as an equal, to be respected as a political human being, and to have no barriers placed in the way of what she can accomplish.

James expressed the heart of the question very well at the conclusion of his letter. "I feel there was a problem with the discussion as a whole," he wrote, "because women comrades were discussed throughout it more as mothers than as leaders of a class or as industrial workers. . . .

"The women comrades in our party are contending for leadership of a class, not just fighting to be accepted by it. We want to help lead—to be a vanguard, not merely assimilate."

The Political Committee affirms or reaffirms three policies with the adoption of this report.

1) The responsibility for child care rests with the individual members who have children, not with the party or other members of the party. Within this framework, the party seeks to help comrades who have children to organize ways to find solutions to the problem of child care that can maximize their participation in political activity.

2) Children should not be present at branch meetings or other meetings that are designed for the conduct of the business of fractions, committees, or other units of the party. Branches should not organize child-care facilities in the headquarters during such meetings.

3) There will be no breast feeding by members at any political meetings or gatherings, including internal party meetings.

Appendix 1
LETTER FROM JAMES, JUNE 12, 1986

Comrades,

On June 1, the St. Louis branch had a two-hour discussion on whether or not a comrade should be allowed to breast feed a child while engaged in party activity. The discussion was initiated by the branch executive committee because Comrade Cris began breast feeding her child at our May 18 branch meeting. At this branch meeting a comrade told Cris that this activity made her feel uncomfortable and that she did not feel it was proper activity for a branch meeting. The comrade then told Cris that she thought it would be better if Cris breast fed her child in the organizer's office where she could listen to the rest of the branch meeting. Cris expressed surprise at this attitude but went into the organizer's office to continue breast feeding the child.

Later that day Cris spoke to me over the telephone and told me that she disagreed with her need to remove herself from the branch meeting when she was breast feeding. I told her then that we should discuss it and until the branch came to a conclusion on it she should do what she thought best.

We did not pursue the point for the next branch meeting because I was out of town for the party plenum, and I asked the executive committee not to take up the point until I had returned. I wanted to be part of the discussion. I also wanted to discuss it a little with the party leadership (which I did briefly). The executive committee agreed to this course of action.

On my returning from the plenum, the executive committee held a discussion and decided that breast feeding in our branch meetings and while on political assignment was inappropriate activity. The exec then delegated Sheila and myself to convey this opinion to Cris and have a discussion with her about it. We did this, and at the meeting Cris explained that she disagreed with the exec's opinion and would like to express her opinion to the branch. We agreed to grant her time to do so. At the branch meeting she was given ten minutes, the same amount of time as the exec reporter.

The basis of the exec report was that since public breast feeding was not a cultural norm in our country and since it was not something we should take a political stance on, that it was inappropriate activity for branch meetings and other political activity and that it contained the possibility of making comrades and others around us uncomfortable. It would draw attention away from our politics. (That it was a distraction.) Also it was pointed out that the branch should take no position on breast feeding as to whether it was progressive or not. And that it was not the purpose of the branch to convince its members to have a more "progressive" stand on the issue. The report also suggested that Cris breast feed in the organizer's office during the branch meetings.

Cris's counterreport basically explained the benefits of breast feeding and suggested that comrades should learn more about it. She also said that the practice of having her breast feed in the organizer's office would exclude her from branch meetings. Thus it would push women away from being able to fully participate in our politics. She also thought comrades were wrong when they stated that this wasn't an accepted practice in North American culture and gave several examples from her own activity to prove differently. She also cited a court case in which a woman won the right to breast feed publicly. Her proposal was that nursing mothers be the ones to decide when and where they would breast feed and that there be no restrictions on it from the branch.

The discussion that followed was long and showed much confused thinking. Almost every comrade present spoke in the discussion. The discussion ended with three-minute summaries.

I proposed that the branch not make any binding decision, retreating from the exec's original proposal, and that we take two straw polls. The first poll was on the gist of the exec report and proposal, and the second on whether comrades thought the decision against breast feeding should not be enforced in a branch meeting but should be prohibited in our public political work (behind a literature table for example). My purpose was to get as clear an idea of how the branch thought on this as possible. On the first vote the result was nine for the exec proposal and nine against, with one abstention. On the second vote the result was 11 for restricting breast feeding while engaged in public political work for the party and seven against it. The branch then voted to bring the discussion to the attention of the national party leadership and ask for help.

One word of explanation. The reason I proposed that the exec retreat from the original position after two hours of discussion was not because I had changed my original opinion, but because of the confused nature of the discussion. Throughout the discussion I barely got the feeling that comrades were discussing the same thing. One group approached the question from the role of the revolutionary party and its cadre in the class and how we present ourselves, and the other from the rights of mothers in the party and how they personally felt about it. The gulf was so wide in the discussion that I thought and still think a binding vote would have been an obstacle to clarification. I think that more discussions are needed on just exactly what a revolutionary party is, so that we could begin from a more common basis. I also thought, and think, that this discussion has to be written up so that comrades can think it through more objectively. And lastly, I was conscious of deciding differently in a local party branch on an issue that is handled differently around the country (including at national party events like YSA conventions and Oberlin).

The discussion in the branch meeting was relatively calm and it has not disrupted other activities. We recently had a good T & P discussion, for example, which is why I am sending this letter in so long after the events. And we've started on our campaign work. There is a great deal of optimism in the branch about its future opportunities to recruit. But still the discussion disturbed comrades on both sides a great deal and must be politically resolved.

There are several points I would like to raise.

Though the discussion was relatively calm, some comrades made statements that the decision on the part of the exec was anti-woman and anti-working class. One comrade said that it was outright reactionary and would prevent us from recruiting women. I think these are pretty grave charges to make even in the heat of a debate. I believe that the comrades believe them.

Another question that disturbed comrades greatly was whether or not we should be discussing this question at all. Most wanted to ignore it at least for the branch meeting. Which is what they encouraged other comrades to do. They felt the discussion was unimportant and an intrusion into a comrade's personal affairs, and it made comrades extremely uncomfortable. I think that the discussion would have been criminal if it had been on what Cris's activities were in her personal life. But this was not the case. What was being questioned was the right of comrades to openly discuss and decide on what goes on in our branch meetings and in our political activity. In effect, what happened was that many of those who professed the most liberal attitudes on breast feeding at any time and any place were the ones who found it the most taboo to discuss openly in the branch. I think that comrades have the right and duty to discuss anything that takes place in the course of our political activity—no matter how seemingly trivial. Many did not agree with this.

Another problem that we had throughout the discussion was the idea that those who were against breast feeding in the branch were backward and those who ignored it or better yet weren't conscious of it were more progressive-thinking; as though being unconscious of something is morally superior to being aware of it. It reminded me of what liberals used to do at some political meetings if someone referred to how many Blacks or whites were in the room. The liberals could always be counted on to say they didn't notice Blacks or whites, they just saw people putting their unconsciousness forward as proof of superiority. This type of reasoning could only work in the party if comrades did not have some feeling that the discussion itself did reflect a backward attitude in the party.

The party's attitude toward children and motherhood, and families, is also very much a part of this discussion. Does the party dislike children? Does it discourage mothers from being members? These questions were reflected more in discussions I had after the branch discussion. Also I am quite sure that some of this is part of a broader discussion on the party among women outside of our ranks. Comrades are very uneasy in explaining the party's attitude on these questions, and some think that the party is somehow anti-baby and wishes to push mothers out or more correctly can't assimilate women with children. The major question is, shouldn't the party make special accommodations or changes for mothers?

There is also a great deal of "claptrap" passed off as science on the best way of raising children. Things the party has no position on. There is a tendency to place the dynamics of the class struggle in second place to good parenting techniques. I bring this up because this became part of our discussion on breast feeding, as to why it was superior to bottle feeding. At this point, the party has no position on this; I don't think it should. But it was this idea that was underlying some of the discussion. I personally think discussions about raising the perfect or near-perfect child have a reactionary tinge to them that places nurturing above the class struggle and tends in the direction of defining women comrades as mothers or nurturers rather than as comrades. After all, if it were true that we could create a better world by raising children better, I think that would be the route to go rather than building the Socialist Workers Party.

I feel there was a problem with the discussion as a whole, because women comrades were discussed throughout it more as mothers than as leaders of a class or as industrial workers. This is partially due, I think in retrospect, to the exec's report. We did not push this aspect of the discussion enough. The women comrades in our party are contending for the leadership of a class, not just fighting to be accepted by it. We want to help lead—to be a vanguard, not merely assimilate. It is not enough for us to argue that breast feeding at public functions will not arouse the contempt of our coworkers (I doubt if it would) or even that it does not make people feel uncomfortable. We have to discuss what we do from the point of view of leading the class and taking ourselves seriously.

This aspect was not discussed enough. The discussion could have been far more concrete and real if comrades had valued their own experiences in the turn more and communicated them.

Lastly, I reject and find dangerous the concept that comrades should be able to function differently in branch meetings than we would in other meetings of our class. I think ideas like this can only tend toward our isolation from the class and make us less confident about recruitment and doing work in the unions and the class as a whole. It also tends in the direction of viewing branch meetings as gatherings of friends in a somewhat larger living room than a serious political meeting.

We encouraged comrades to write down what they thought on this and send the letters to the Organization Bureau. These are my thoughts on the discussion. The executive committee no longer has a position separate from the branch on this matter. As it stands now the branch has no position other than to allow individual comrades to make their own decisions.

Comradely,
/s/
James

LETTER FROM VIVIAN, JUNE 6, 1986

Dear Comrades,

A discussion has come up in the St. Louis branch about breast feeding during political activities.

Three weeks ago, just as our branch meeting was about to begin, Cris started to breast feed her child in our meeting room. I told her that I was very surprised, that I had assumed that she would go to some private area such as the bathroom to breast feed. Cris was very surprised that I raised this; she told me that she had thought me "progressive." She said she had breast fed her child the day before at our educational conference, and that in her opinion public breast feeding was acceptable whether at branch meetings, forums, or literature tables; that it was a question for individual mothers to decide. She also told me that a woman had been arrested for indecent exposure for breast feeding in her car in St. Louis recently and that she had won the case.

Since I disagreed that public breast feeding was a cultural norm in our country, we both decided that the branch would have to take up this question and Cris agreed to breast feed in the organizer's office for that particular branch meeting.

The branch executive committee discussed this and at the June 1 branch meeting proposed that comrades not breast feed while carrying out public party activities and that during party meetings in the hall, that comrades go to the organizer's office.

Cris gave a separate report on the question and proposed that she be the one to decide where she breast feeds.

Our branch decided to ask for some help from the Organization Bureau in thinking this out. We took a straw vote on the executive committee's proposal that went nine for, nine against, and one abstention. Cris asked for a second straw vote, which said it was okay to breast feed at internal party meetings but taking no position on breast feeding on public party assignment. This passed with 11 yes votes, seven against, and one abstention.

In this letter I would like to make a few comments on the branch discussion.

First, on the idea that even if it might not be right to breast feed while publicly representing the party, it is okay at branch meetings. Comrades, it was said, can get used to it or just not look.

My question is why we would want to do things in branch meetings that we wouldn't be comfortable with in union meetings? How can we fit this idea with the idea that we want to recruit new people to our party? Will we be more confident in asking people to join our party if it means that we'll be asking them to come to meetings where we have different norms of conduct? Do we have a "public" face and a "private" one? Are we, who are already in the party, some advanced breed, or are we a political party made up of people who work together based on a particular set of political ideas and goals? If we are serious about being a revolutionary party, a party that strives to lead the masses of working people and farmers in taking state power away from U.S. imperialism, don't we have to be very serious about any question that might be an obstacle in our path?

On a second point—I think we could use some more discussion on why branches take up issues like this. A big part of Cris's report to the branch was on the benefits of breast feeding.

The pros and cons of breast feeding became part of our discussion. One comrade said that the executive committee's proposal reflected the party's isolation from children and childraising. Another said that there was a "new trend" in breast feeding in the women's movement, a trend over the last 5–7 years that the branch should catch up to.

A lot more than nutritional considerations were raised. Part of the trend, according to Cris, is public breast feeding. She told the branch that she had nursed walking through a department store and that only one child had commented on the fact to her mother. Another trend, she told me, was to nurse for longer periods. Some women she knew were nursing children till they were four or five years old. She urged the branch to read various books on this question to get educated on it.

I want to express my opinion here—that the party should not take a position for or against breast feeding.

Sometimes breast feeding is a political issue. We ran articles, I believe, in *Intercontinental Press* when women in underdeveloped countries led a campaign against the Nestlé's corporation because they did not have access to clean drinking water for baby formula—something the profit-hungry company didn't care a thing about. (This example was raised by a comrade in the branch to show that breast feeding is progressive.)

On the other hand, it strikes me, at least, that in this country recent articles about the benefits of breast feeding have run alongside articles about the benefits of staying home with the kids instead of putting them in child-care centers. A sort of "be there for your child" package.

I don't know if more working-class women are breast feeding today. It's certainly not a new invention. I do doubt if many working-class women have the option of breast feeding for years at a time. Perhaps it is only something else for us working mothers to feel guilty about.

For the future, I think that what our party is fighting for is a society where individual mothers can have real options based on the best medical knowledge. A future where a great deal about the relations between mothers and children will be looked at with a fresh eye.

There is one other point that came up in the branch meeting that I would appreciate more discussion on.

That's the problem that if the branch asks a comrade to breast feed in the organizer's office during a branch meeting or forum, then we are limiting that comrade's ability to fully participate in the party.

Some comrades express the opinion that such a decision would be "anti-woman" and/or "anti-working class."

Thinking back over the last 13 years in the SWP with my three children, I can think of many, many times where I had to make decisions about my political activities that were affected by my having children. Many decisions I've made have affected them too—the job changes I've made, the times I've transferred from one city to another. And my children have not always been happy with my decisions.

But one of the things I most appreciated about the party when I first came around it was that in contrast to the rest of the world that was telling me all the things I couldn't do because now I had to be a responsible parent, the party opened doors to me the same way it did to every other comrade and put no limits on my participation.

We have to put the best interest of the party first. We are all asked to subordinate personal plans towards building the party. Comrades who are mothers, with the very real burdens that places on us, have to contribute to the party to the best of our abilities.

I also question whether having a comrade breast feed while carrying out political work is actually allowing her to participate fully.

Women who want to be taken seriously politically, who strive to be leaders of both the men and women in our country, have to consider how we present ourselves.

Would we expect any woman in our party to stand up and give a political report while nursing, or is there just a layer that it's acceptable for?

How many discussions have we had about the problem of selling *Militant*s when men try to flirt with us instead of listening to us. It's a discussion that comes up at work too, and not just for comrades. Especially in non-traditional jobs women do think out how we present ourselves, aware of the prejudices that exist against us.

I wouldn't expect that coworkers would be contemptuous of a woman who breast feeds at union meetings, but I don't know if she would stand out as someone you'd turn to for class leadership. Would you have her be your press spokesperson?

I've always found Castro's decision to keep his personal life out of politics rather interesting. It has always struck me that on a new job the first thing people want to find out about a new woman worker is her family situation—it is such an overwhelming thing in our society to define women by such matters. I've even heard comrades say that they feel pressure because they don't have kids and "look different." I think that is part of dividing our class—to keep women looking at themselves in these terms.

I think it's the 180 degree opposite from being "anti-woman" or "anti-working class" to expect our women members to consider these questions, when we expect them to be leaders of our party.

Comradely,
/s/
Vivian

Appendix 2

EXCERPT FROM REPORT ON WOMEN'S LIBERATION MOVEMENT
Adopted by SWP National Committee, March 14, 1971

by Betsey Stone

There is another question I want to take up in relation to the party, and this is child care for party members and sympathizers with children. We want parents, both female and male comrades, with children to be active in the revolutionary movement. We realize that parents face extra difficulties and burdens in this society because of the lack of social facilities for the care of children. Traditionally, most of these extra burdens have fallen on women, and have especially discouraged women with children from participating fully in revolutionary activity.

There are a number of concrete things we can do, and are doing, in this regard. We can encourage cooperation between parents to watch each other's children during party activities, we can provide facilities where children can be watched by parents or volunteers at party conventions or other important party functions such as branch meetings. Individual comrades can volunteer to watch the children of other comrades, to free them, if necessary, for party work.

In instances where the party has been able to afford it, comrades with children who have worked for the party full time have received extra expense money to help meet the additional financial burden.

At the same time, we approach the problem of child care with the understanding that the question of whether or not people have children, or how they raise them, is *not* a party matter, but a personal one. Raising children is very time consuming, and it will continue to be so until a successful social revolution is able to provide the necessary resources for full time child care facilities for everyone.

In the meantime, the party itself cannot take responsibility for the care of comrades' children.

The party itself cannot make up for, or solve, the enormous social inequities and problems created by capitalism. This applies to many things in addition to child care—like unemployment, medical care, housing, education, etc. We do whatever possible to help comrades solve such problems, but we cannot make the party responsible for solving them.

When the question of providing child care during branch activities comes up, it must be considered carefully, according to the concrete situation. Are there adequate facilities where children can play or will their presence disrupt the branch activity? What can be gained by making facilities available, and asking for volunteers to watch children? Are there alternative solutions?

Whatever decision is made, participation by comrades in staffing the child care facilities must be voluntary. That is comrades cannot be required or obligated to take care of other comrades' children. To do so would create all kinds of problems and resentments against those comrades with children. If the branch were responsible for taking care of comrades' children, branch members would begin to feel the party should have some say over whether people have children or not.

That may sound strange, but I have seen problems of this kind develop, especially in smaller branches with few people to take care of all the branch responsibilities. In one branch, when a number of comrades became pregnant, other comrades resented very much the extra burden they feared would be imposed on the branch in caring for the children.

The question of providing child care for non-SWP functions, or functions open to the public, is more complicated. We certainly should help with child care at women's liberation conferences, antiwar conferences, and other public events where it is decided that it would be good to provide these facilities. But, we must also be very careful when we take responsibility for other people's children. In functions sponsored by the SWP, we must be especially careful that proper care will be provided for the children, and that competent comrades are in charge. A lot of people don't know anything about caring for children. They panic when faced with a screaming or crying child. Or their negligence, or lack of experience, could cause a child to get hurt. Non-members might resent the party for this, or we could even get into a situation where the party could be sued by such a parent.

Before any decisions are made, or drifted into, the benefits to the party should be concretely weighed against the time and energy expended. If it is decided to provide facilities in some cases, they should be adequate, staffed by volunteer personnel, and competent people should be responsible.

From Pathfinder

Are They Rich Because They're Smart?
Class, Privilege, and Learning under Capitalism
JACK BARNES

In battles forced on us by the capitalists, workers will begin to transform our attitudes toward life, work, and each other. We'll discover our worth, denied by the rulers and upper middle classes who insist they're rich because they're smart. We'll learn in struggle what we're capable of becoming. $10. Also in Spanish, French, and Farsi.

In Defense of the US Working Class
MARY-ALICE WATERS

A giant has begun to stir. Hillary Clinton calls them "deplorables" living in "backward" parts of the US. But tens of thousands of teachers and school employees in 2018 waged victorious strikes. Working people in Florida won restoration of voting rights to former prisoners. In doing so, they drew on the best fighting traditions of workers of all skin colors and national origins. $7. Also in Spanish and Farsi.

Malcolm X, Black Liberation, and the Road to Workers Power
JACK BARNES

Why the conquest of power by the working class will make possible the final battle for Black freedom—and open the way to a world based on human solidarity, not exploitation, violence, and racism. A socialist world. $20. Also in Spanish, French, Farsi, Arabic, and Greek.

The Origin of the Family, Private Property, and the State
FREDERICK ENGELS

How the emergence of class-divided society gave rise to repressive state bodies and family structures that protect the property of the ruling layers and enable them to pass along wealth and privilege. Engels discusses the consequences for working people of these class institutions—from their original forms to their modern versions. $18. Also in Farsi.

The Clintons' Anti-Working-Class Record
Why Washington Fears Working People
JACK BARNES

The profit-driven course of Democrats and Republicans alike since the White House of William and Hillary Clinton in the 1990s, and the political awakening of workers seeking to understand and resist these assaults. $10. Also in Spanish, French, and Farsi.

Women's Liberation and the African Freedom Struggle
THOMAS SANKARA

"There is no true social revolution without the liberation of women," explains the leader of the 1983–87 revolution in the West African country of Burkina Faso. $8. Also in Spanish, French, and Farsi.

WOMEN'S LIBERATION AND SOCIALISM

Women in Cuba: The Making of a Revolution within the Revolution
VILMA ESPÍN, ASELA DE LOS SANTOS, YOLANDA FERRER

The integration of women into the ranks and leadership of the Cuban Revolution was inseparably intertwined with the proletarian course of the revolution from the start. This is the story of that revolution and how it transformed the women and men who made it. $20. Also in Spanish and Greek.

Feminism and the Marxist Movement
MARY-ALICE WATERS

Since the founding of the modern revolutionary workers movement nearly 150 years ago, Marxists have championed the struggle for women's rights and explained the economic roots in class society of women's oppression. "The struggle for women's liberation," Waters writes, "was lifted out of the realm of the personal, the 'impossible dream,' and unbreakably linked to the progressive forces of our epoch"—the working-class struggle for power. $6. Also in Farsi.

Marianas in Combat
Teté Puebla and the Mariana Grajales Women's Platoon in Cuba's Revolutionary War 1956–58
TETÉ PUEBLA

Brigadier General Teté Puebla, the highest ranking woman in Cuba's Revolutionary Armed Forces, joined the struggle to overthrow the US-backed dictatorship of Fulgencio Batista in 1956, when she was fifteen years old. This is her story—from clandestine action in the cities, to serving as an officer in the victorious Rebel Army's first all-women's unit. The fight to transform the social and economic status of women in Cuba remains inseparable from its socialist revolution. $14. Also in Spanish and Farsi.

Woman's Evolution
From Matriarchal Clan to Patriarchal Family
EVELYN REED

Assesses women's leading and still largely unknown contributions to the development of human civilization and refutes the myth that women have always been subordinate to men. "Certain to become a classic text in women's history"—*Publishers Weekly*. $32. Also in Farsi.

Abortion Is a Woman's Right!
PAT GROGAN, EVELYN REED

Why abortion rights are central not only to the fight for the full emancipation of women, but to forging a united and fighting labor movement. $6. Also in Spanish.

Women and the Family
LEON TROTSKY

How the October 1917 Russian Revolution, the first victorious socialist revolution, opened the door to new possibilities in the fight for women's liberation. $13

Sexism and Science
EVELYN REED

Are human beings innately aggressive? Does biology condemn women to remain the "second sex"? Taking up such biases cloaked as the findings of science, Reed explains that the disciplines closest to human life—anthropology, biology, and sociology—are permeated with rationalizations for the oppression of women and the maintenance of the established capitalist order. $20. Also in Farsi.

Capital
KARL MARX

The best book ever written on the oppression of women, their exploitation in modern society, and the road to emancipation. Volume 1, $18; volume 2, $18; volume 3, $18.

WWW.PATHFINDERPRESS.COM

EXPAND YOUR REVOLUTIONARY LIBRARY

The History of American Trotskyism, 1928–38
Report of a Participant
JAMES P. CANNON

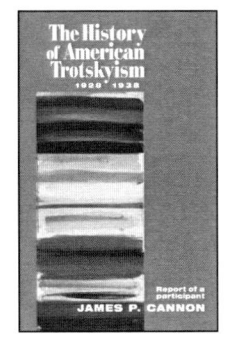

"Trotskyism is not a new movement, a new doctrine," Cannon says, "but the restoration, the revival of genuine Marxism as it was expounded and practiced in the Russian Revolution and in the early days of the Communist International." Talks by a founding leader of American communism on building a proletarian party in the United States. $22. Also in Spanish and French.

How Far We Slaves Have Come!
South Africa and Cuba in Today's World
NELSON MANDELA, FIDEL CASTRO

Cuban internationalists "made a contribution to African independence, freedom, and justice, unparalleled for its principles and selfless character," said Nelson Mandela, speaking in Cuba in July 1991 alongside Fidel Castro. Here are their speeches on the victory by Cuban, Angolan, and Namibian combatants over the US-backed South African army that had invaded Angola. $10. Also in Spanish and Farsi.

Trade Unions in the Epoch of Imperialist Decay
LEON TROTSKY, FARRELL DOBBS, KARL MARX

Food for thought—and action—from revolutionary leaders of three different generations of the modern working-class movement. Invaluable to the practical education of militant workers relearning today what a strike is and how it can be fought and won. $16

Is Biology Woman's Destiny?
EVELYN REED

The roots of women's oppression as a "second sex." $5. Also in Farsi and Arabic.

Puerto Rico: Independence Is a Necessity
RAFAEL CANCEL MIRANDA

One of the five Puerto Rican Nationalists imprisoned by Washington for more than 25 years and released in 1979 speaks out on the brutal reality of US colonial domination, the campaign to free Puerto Rican political prisoners, the example of Cuba's socialist revolution, and the ongoing struggle for independence. $6. Also in Spanish and Farsi.

Malcolm X Talks to Young People

"The young generation of whites, Blacks, browns, whatever else there is—you're living at a time of revolution," Malcolm said in December 1964. "And I for one will join in with anyone, I don't care what color you are, as long as you want to change this miserable condition that exists on this earth." $15. Also in Spanish, French, Farsi, and Greek.

Socialism on Trial
Testimony at Minneapolis Sedition Trial
JAMES P. CANNON

The revolutionary program of the working class, as presented in response to frame-up charges of "seditious conspiracy" in 1941, on the eve of US entry into World War II. The defendants were leaders of the Minneapolis labor movement and the Socialist Workers Party. $16. Also in Spanish, French, and Farsi.

Fighting Racism in World War II
FROM THE PAGES OF THE *MILITANT*

An account of struggles against racist discrimination in US war industries, the armed forces, and society as a whole from 1939 to 1945, taken from the pages of the socialist newsweekly, the *Militant*. These struggles helped lay the basis for the proletarian-based civil rights movement that followed. $25

Teamster Bureaucracy
FARRELL DOBBS

How class-conscious workers led labor opposition to US imperialism's entry into World War II. And how Washington, aided by the Teamster bureaucracy, used the FBI to try to smash union power and gag antiwar views. Now with more than 130 photos and illustrations. $19. Also in Spanish.

"It's the Poor Who Face the Savagery of the US 'Justice' System"
The Cuban Five Talk about Their Lives within the US Working Class

How US cops, courts, and prisons work as "an enormous machine for grinding people up." Five Cuban revolutionaries framed up and held in US jails for 16 years explain the human devastation of capitalist "justice"—and how socialist Cuba is different. $15. Also in Spanish, Farsi, and Greek.

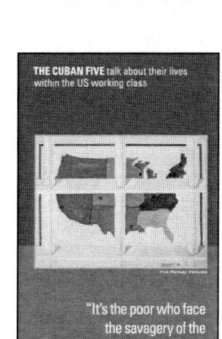

Capitalism's Long Hot Winter Has Begun
JACK BARNES

Published as the storm clouds of the 2008 financial crisis were forming, Barnes explains that today's global capitalist crisis is but the opening stage of decades of economic, financial, and social convulsions and class battles. Class-conscious workers, he writes, confront this historic turning point for imperialism with confidence, drawing satisfaction from being "in their face" as we chart a revolutionary course to take power. In *New International* no. 12. $16. Also in Spanish, French, Farsi, Arabic, and Greek.

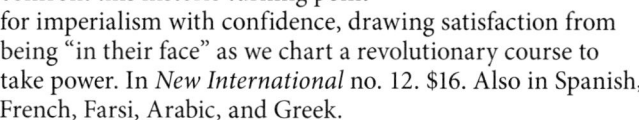

Is Socialist Revolution in the US Possible?
A Necessary Debate among Working People
MARY-ALICE WATERS

An unhesitating "Yes"—that's the answer given here. Possible—but not inevitable. That depends on what working people *do*. $10. Also in Spanish, French, and Farsi.

To See the Dawn
Baku, 1920—First Congress of the Peoples of the East

How can peasants and workers in the colonial world achieve freedom from imperialist exploitation? By what means can working people overcome divisions incited by their national ruling classes and act together for their common class interests? These questions were addressed by 2,000 delegates to the 1920 Congress of the Peoples of the East. $24

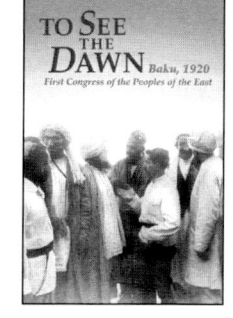

Maurice Bishop Speaks
The Grenada Revolution and its Overthrow, 1979–83

The triumph of the 1979 revolution in the Caribbean island of Grenada under the leadership of Maurice Bishop gave hope to millions throughout the Americas. Invaluable lessons from the workers and farmers government defeated by a Stalinist-led coup in 1983. $25

The History of the Russian Revolution
LEON TROTSKY

How, under Lenin's leadership, the Bolshevik Party led millions of workers and farmers to overthrow the state power of the landlords and capitalists in 1917 and bring to power a government that advanced their class interests at home and worldwide. Unabridged, 3 vols. in one. Written by one of the central leaders of that socialist revolution. $38. Also in French and Russian.

Revolutionary Continuity
Marxist Leadership in the United States
FARRELL DOBBS

"Successive generations of proletarian revolutionaries have participated in the movements of the working class and its allies and sought to steer them along the correct path.... Marxists today owe them not only homage for their deeds. We also have a duty to learn where they went wrong as well as what they did right so their errors are not repeated."
—*Farrell Dobbs*

2 volumes: *The Early Years, 1848–1917*, $16; *Birth of the Communist Movement, 1918–1922*, $16.

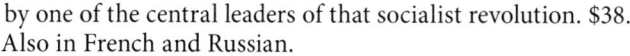

WWW.PATHFINDERPRESS.COM

Capitalism's World Disorder
Working-Class Politics at the Millennium
JACK BARNES

The social devastation and financial crises, the coarsening of politics, the cop brutality and acts of imperialist aggression accelerating around us—all are products not of something gone wrong with capitalism but of its lawful workings. Yet the future can be changed by the united struggle and selfless action of working people conscious of their power to transform the world. $25. Also in Spanish and French.

Cuba and the Coming American Revolution
JACK BARNES

This is a book about the struggles of working people in the imperialist heartland, the youth attracted to them, and the example set by the Cuban people that revolution is not only necessary—it can be made. It is about the class struggle in the US, where the revolutionary capacities of workers and farmers are today as utterly discounted by the ruling powers as were those of the Cuban toilers. And just as wrongly. $10. Also in Spanish, French, and Farsi.

Thomas Sankara Speaks
The Burkina Faso Revolution, 1983–87

Under Sankara's guidance, Burkina Faso's revolutionary government led peasants, workers, women, and youth to expand literacy; to sink wells, plant trees, erect housing; to combat women's oppression; to carry out land reform; to join others in Africa and worldwide to free themselves from the imperialist yoke. $24. Also in French.

50 Years of Covert Operations in the US
Washington's Political Police and the American Working Class
LARRY SEIGLE, FARRELL DOBBS, STEVE CLARK

How class-conscious workers have fought against the drive to build the "national security" state essential to maintaining capitalist rule. $12. Also in Spanish and Farsi.

U.S. Imperialism Has Lost the Cold War
JACK BARNES

The collapse of regimes across Eastern Europe and the USSR claiming to be communist did not mean workers and farmers there had been defeated. In today's sharpening capitalist conflicts and wars, these toilers are an intractable obstacle to the profit system's advance, gaining leadership experience as they fight. In *New International* no. 11. $16. Also in Spanish, French, Farsi, and Greek.

The Revolution Betrayed
What is the Soviet Union and Where Is It Going?
LEON TROTSKY

In 1917 workers and peasants of Russia were the motor force for one of the deepest revolutions in history. Yet within ten years a political counterrevolution by a privileged social layer whose chief spokesperson was Joseph Stalin was being consolidated. The classic study of the Soviet workers state and its degeneration. $20. Also in Spanish, Farsi, and Greek.

Their Trotsky and Ours
JACK BARNES

To lead the working class in a successful revolution, a mass proletarian party is needed whose cadres, well beforehand, have absorbed a world communist program, are proletarian in life and work, derive deep satisfaction from doing politics, and have forged a leadership with an acute sense of what to do next. This book is about building such a party. $16. Also in Spanish, French, and Farsi.

The Fight against Fascism in the USA
Forty Years of Struggle Described by Participants
JAMES P. CANNON, OTHERS

Lessons from the fight against incipient fascist movements since the capitalist crisis and labor radicalization of the 1930s. $12